The UK Air Fryer

Cookbook for Beginners

Delicious & Easy-to-Follow Breakfast, Lunch,

and Dinner Recipes for Brits Only

Archie Peacock

Contents

Introduction

Air fryers are versatile and handy devices that can help you cook a variety of foods - from potatoes and chicken nuggets to zucchini slices - with little to no oil. They work by circulating heated air around the food, cooking it evenly and creating a crispy outer layer while keeping the inside soft - just like deep-fried foods. And since the air fryer cooks the food by circulating hot air around it, any grease that drips off is caught in a container below the basket, making it a healthier option than traditional deep frying. So if you're looking for a convenient and healthier way to fry foods, an air fryer is a great choice! This cooking method not only cuts down on harmful effects of oil frying, but it also lowers the amount of acrylamide in fried potatoes by 90%. Acrylamide is a chemical that is linked to greater chances of getting cancer, and it is produced when you fry potatoes or other starchy foods.

Do you want to cook with less oil? Air fryers are a great option because they circulate hot air very efficiently to create a "fried finish" on food with little to no oil. This is something that is tricky to achieve in an oven. Additionally, the compact size of air fryers means they cook ingredients quickly. Plus, they are more energy efficient than turning on your oven for cooking smaller quantities. This can save you time and money on your energy bills. Most air fryers are compact enough to fit on a kitchen countertop, making them a healthier alternative to deep-fat fryers. But what can you cook in an air fryer? Air fried chicken, buffalo cauliflower "wings", air fryer baked potatoes, air fryer doughnuts, kale chips and traditional chips can all be made with air crisp functions. But look out for reheat, baking, roasting, dehydrating and grilling functions which open up the option to cook entire meals, plus pudding!

An air fryer is a versatile and convenient kitchen appliance that can cook, roast, bake, broil, crisp, dehydrate and reheat foods with little to no oil. It's easy to use, and once you get the hang of it you'll be hooked on air frying! There are two main types of air fryers: basket air fryers and air fryer ovens. Basket air fryers have a removable basket in which you put food. Air fryer ovens look similar to a toaster oven and have racks inside on which you put food. Air fryer ovens typically have more cooking functions and more room for food inside, but they also take up more space in your kitchen.

What is Air Fryer?

Air fryers are large countertop appliances that offer a bold promise: perfectly fried food using very little oil (often less than a tablespoon). Despite the clever name, an air fryer is not a fryer at all. It's a mini convection oven that cook food by circulating hot air around it with a fan. This way, food is cooked by convection, which means it can approach the crispiness of fried food while using far less oil. But the intense hot air is also ideal for roasting and even allows you to prepare dishes you might otherwise cook on the grill.

The air fryer does what it's supposed to do: You can cook with very little oil and still get crisp, French fry-like results. But we found that the results are more like oven-fried food, rather than deep-fried food. This is because deep frying requires a lot of

fat for that "fried" flavor, and air-fried or oven-fried foods taste leaner in comparison. Even so, we found that the best air fryers produced food that tasted even better than oven-fried foods.

What Type of Air Fryers Are There?

Basket style with heating elements: Air fryers come in all shapes and sizes, but the most popular ones are tall and slim with a main unit that houses the heating elements and fans. These fryers also have slide-out baskets or trays that fit snugly into place inside. Because they typically have a smaller cooking area than oven-style fryers, we found that even results were more likely if the cooking was paused occasionally to rearrange or toss the food around. Some fryers will cut out automatically when you do this, while others will need to be paused manually if you want accurate timings.

Rotisserie air fryers: These rotisserie baskets are designed to cook chicken evenly and quickly, while still maintaining moisture. The interior lights also make it a great option for entertaining guests. Plus, the baskets can also be used to cook potatoes - just add them in raw and they'll come out crispy thanks to the even heat distribution.

"Mini oven" types: These models utilize convection or fan technology to cook food evenly on flat, slide-in trays. In addition to roasting, the extra air frying functions circulating hot air around the food helps make it crispier. These usually took up the space of an average-sized microwave. Some may also include rotisserie elements.

Interior paddles: Some air fryers have an internal paddle that causes a stirring motion which in turn keeps the food circulating around a doughnut-shaped tray. Unlike 'basket' models, the oil stays in the pan which means that this appliance can also be used for cooking sauces, rice, or casserole-type recipes.

What Can You Cook in an Air Fryer?

When it comes to recipes, air fryers are great for not only making your favorite traditional dishes, but for helping you experiment with new things as well. A great place to start is with the humble potato. As we mention above, it's possible to achieve a similar texture and flavor of traditional fried potatoes (like chips and roasted potatoes) using the air-crisp function on your air fryer, but with considerably less oil. The same goes for coated foods that you want to be crispy on the outside, like breadcrumbs. Explore our collection of air fryer recipes for some inspiration on how to make delicious air-fried vegetables and chicken.

Many mid-range models come with the option to bake, and usually come with non-stick accessories. This means you can experiment with different kinds of baking, like classic cake recipes or free-from options for people with dietary requirements. Fruit leather is a great way to use a dehydrate function, and if you have a hand blender, blender or food processor at home, you can make it yourself. You can also try dehydrating tomatoes or mushrooms for an umami flavor.

How to Use an Air Fryer?

There are exceptional tips with aid you to have yummiest meal with perfection.

Don't overcrowd the basket
To ensure that your food cooks evenly and comes out crispy, be sure to cook it in a single layer in the air fryer basket. You can cook in batches as necessary. And if you want to check on the progress of your food during cooking, it's perfectly fine to open the basket and take a look!

Choose the right temperature
A rule of thumb when cooking with an air fryer is to lower the temperature by 25 degrees in comparison to if you were cooking the same food in an oven. Many air fryers come with manuals that recommend temperatures for different types of food, but if you're unsure, it's always best to follow recipes from trusted sources. I've included some links to my favorite tried-and-true air fryer recipes below.

Shake or flip part way through to cook evenly
It's important to shake the basket when cooking small pieces of food so that they cook evenly and brown nicely. For meat, flipping it over halfway through the cooking time will help it cook evenly as well.

Dry foods well to get them crispy
Before you add oil, seasonings, or place your food in the air fryer basket, make sure to pat it dry with a clean kitchen towel or paper towels. Moisture is the enemy of crispiness, and you'll want to avoid it if you're aiming for a delicious and crispy meal!

Air frying presets
While many air fryers come with preset programs that have cook times and temperatures for common foods, I find that I prefer to use the manual air fry function. This allows me to set the cook time and temperature myself according to what I'm cooking.

Step-By-Step Air Frying

You must preheat your air fryer before you start cooking. This is because when you preheat the air fryer, the food will cook at a higher temperature, giving you a crispy exterior. Most air fryers have a preheat button that you can press to start the preheating process. But for some cheaper, small air fryers, you will have to preheat manually. To do this, heat the air fryer to 400°F for 5 minutes.

The air fryer preheats quickly, so once it's done, take the basket out and put the food inside. Make sure not to overload the basket, though, as this will make the food cook unevenly.

After placing your food items into the air fryer basket, insert the basket into the air fryer. You will then need to set the appropriate time and temperature for your meal. Although, you can always change the time and temperature settings during the cooking process if necessary.

To begin air frying, press the start button. Once you've started cooking, it's important to make sure the food doesn't get overcooked or burnt. To ensure this, mix the food contents in the middle of the cooking process or turn the food upside down. The air fryer will beep when the cooking time is finished.

Then, take out the air fryer basket. Be careful of the hot steam. Separate the inner basket from the outer basket and serve the food. However, when separating the inner basket from the outer basket, keep the basket on a flat surface. The basket must completely cool down before cleaning.

Straight from the Store

Before using the air fryer for the first time, you must remove all stickers and packaging. Next, place the fryer on a sturdy, heat-resistant surface away from any other objects or surfaces to prevent damage from steam.

To remove the plastic packaging, use the handle to take out the basket and release the button to separate the inner and outer baskets.

Thoroughly clean both baskets using either a dishwasher or non-abrasive sponge. Wipe down the inside and outside of the basket with a slightly damp cloth, and use a dry towel to dry the basket before putting it back in the air fryer.

Cleaning and Caring for Your Air Fryer

Cleaning your air fryer is important to keep it functioning properly and looking great. Most air fryers have a nonstick coating that helps to make clean up easy. Most basket-style air fryers have an inner and outer basket that can be taken apart for washing.

You can wash the basket in warm, soapy water. Be sure to use a non-abrasive cloth or sponge so as not to damage the nonstick coating. You can check your instruction manual to see if the baskets for your model of air fryer are dishwasher safe, but I recommend hand washing because the parts should wash up easily and it may make them last longer.

For the quickest and easiest clean-up, rinse the basket right after cooking.

The removable parts of an oven-style air fryer can be cleaned with warm soapy water or in the dishwasher. If the surface of the air fryer base unit gets dirty, wipe it clean with a soft, damp cloth.

You can put aluminum foil or parchment paper in the air fryer, and there are even sheets of perforated parchment paper designed specifically for air fryer use. The holes in the paper allow air to circulate while cooking. However, never run your air fryer with parchment paper or foil in it without food on top of the paper/foil, as the paper may lift up and touch the heating element otherwise.

Benefits of Using It

Healthier Cooking
The main reason people invest in an air fryer is for the prospect of healthier cooking. By using little to no oil in the cooking process, it's the perfect way to gradually phase out deep fried foods that aren't very healthy.

Fast, Safe and Easy to Use
The air fryer was designed to be a replacement for the deep fryer. we'd all love to cook more often, but we don't have the time to do so. This is why ready meals and takeaway are popular, even when we know they're unhealthy.

Crisp & Crunchy Food
The air fryer is perfect for anyone who loves cooking frozen or breaded foods like chicken tenders and onion rings. The air fryer will actually crisp up the food, so you won't end up with a soggy mess. All you need is a little bit of spray cooking oil on the outside of the food and you'll be left with a crunchy and golden exterior.

It's Very Versatile
The air fryer is more than just a healthier alternative to deep frying; you can cook almost anything in it, it's also great for cooking frozen foods like French fries, tater tots, and pizza rolls. So easy that the kids can even do it. That's dinner, sorted.

Faster than Oven Cooking
An air fryer has many advantages, one being that it heats up quickly and the circulating air helps the food cook evenly, get browned and crispy - all with little to no intervention. This means you can cut down your cook time significantly.

Reheat Foods with Ease
Not only can you cook meals quickly and easily in an air fryer, but reheating food in the air fryer is a great way to make it even more delicious.

Easy to Clean
A good air fryer is not only easy to use, but also easy to clean - meaning you can spend less time scrubbing away and more time enjoying your delicious meal.

Air Fryer Cooking Tips

When cooking fatty foods, add water to the air fryer drawer. Adding water to the drawer underneath the basket helps prevent grease from getting too hot and smoking. Do this when cooking bacon, sausage, even burgers if they are particularly fatty.

Don't overcrowd the basket. I can't stress this enough. It's tempting to try to cook more at one time, but over-crowding the basket will prevent foods from crisping and browning evenly and take more time over all. So cook in batches if you need to!

Flip foods over halfway through the cooking time to ensure even browning. Just as you would if cooking on a grill or in a skillet, you need to turn foods over so that they brown evenly.

Open the air fryer as often as you like to check for doneness. This is one of the great things about air fryers – you can open that drawer as often as you like (within reason) to check on the cooking process. This will not interrupt the timing of most air fryers – the fryer will either continue heating and timing as you pull the basket out.

Use toothpicks to secure light foods. Every once in a while, the fan from the air fryer can pick up light foods and blow them around. So, to avoid this, use toothpicks to hold down items like the top slice of bread on a sandwich.

Shake the basket a couple of times during cooking. This will help to re-distribute the ingredients and ensure that they brown and crisp more evenly.

Spritzing your food with oil partway through the cooking process will help it to brown and crisp more evenly. If you're trying to get your food to brown and crisp more, spraying it with oil partway through the cooking process is the way to go!

Before removing the air fryer basket, make sure to turn out the food first. This is very important to avoid making a big mess. If you invert the basket while it is still locked into the air fryer drawer, all the rendered fat or excess grease will end up dumping onto your plate along with the food you just air-fried.

The drawer below the air fryer basket collects a lot of flavorful juices from the cooked foods above, which can make an excellent sauce to pour over your food. If the drippings are not too greasy, you can de-grease them and reduce them in a small saucepan on the stovetop for a few minutes to concentrate the flavor. This will make a delicious and healthy addition to your meal.

It's important to clean the drawer and basket of your air fryer after each use. The drawer is easy to clean, so there's no excuse for putting it off. If you don't wash it, you could contaminate your food and make your kitchen smell bad.

The air fryer has a self-cleaning feature that is both easy and effective. To clean the air fryer basket and drawer, simply put them back in the air fryer and turn it on for 2-3 minutes. The heat generated will dry both parts more thoroughly than any drying towel.

Are Air Fryers Healthy?

Here are five reasons why an air fryer is a healthier choice than many other ways of cooking.

An air fryer cuts calories by up to 80%
An air fryer is a healthier alternative to deep frying because it can cut calories by up to 80%. This kitchen appliance is perfect for those who are looking to reduce their calorie and fat intake. Air fryers are also a great option for making fried snacks at home. This is especially beneficial if you're trying to avoid takeout from your favorite restaurant.

Air fryers offer a lower fat way of frying
If you want to keep eating fried foods but want to be healthier, then an air fryer is the way to go. Air fryers cook food by heating it in hot air that has small droplets of oil in it. This means that the fat intake is lower than deep fat frying. Air fryers are also healthier than shallow frying. Putting food in a basket or tray with holes lets any oil from the food drain as it cooks. The oil collects underneath the basket or tray and can be thrown away.

Air frying lowers levels of acrylamide
Acrylamide is a known carcinogen, which is often found in starchy foods. Lowering the level of acrylamide is always a healthier option. When compared to cooking in oil, air frying at high temperatures helps to lower the levels of acrylamide found in starchy foods, like potatoes.

Air frying helps to preserve nutrients
Air frying has been shown in some studies to help preserve certain nutrients, like vitamin C and polyphenols. Convection heating - which is what air fryers use - helps to keep nutrients from being lost during cooking. Additionally, convection cooking often speeds up the cooking process overall and provides a crispier finish to whatever food you're making.

Air fryers are more eco-friendly
Air fryers have many advantages over traditional ovens, one of which is their smaller size. They also heat up very quickly, which is perfect for those who want to have their food fried without the long wait. The hot air circulates quickly around the oven, browning and crisping the food so that it looks like it was fried - even though it wasn't! This is a much safer method than deep fat frying, as there is no risk of spilling hot oil or starting a fire.

You can cook without any oil
You may not believe it, but you can actually cook without using any oil in an air fryer. This is because the hot air convection helps to speed up the cooking process, without the need for oil. So, if you're looking to cut back on the amount of oil and fat in your food, air fryers are a great option for crisping it up, without submerging it in fat.

Frequently Asked Questions

Do I need to preheat my air fryer?
The quick answer is no; you don't need to preheat your air fryer. In fact, one of the advantages of using an air fryer is that it heats up much faster than an oven. So when you're developing recipes for your air fryer cookbook, Air Fryer Perfection, you'll

find that the total time it takes to cook food starts in a cold air fryer is the same as when you wait a few minutes for the air fryer to heat up and then add your food. Plus, skipping the preheating step is convenient. So there you have it - one less thing to worry about when using your air fryer!

How much can an air fryer hold?

Generally speaking, most air fryers can fit enough food for 2 to 4 people, depending on the type of food. It's important not to overcrowd the basket, as this can lead to uneven cooking. If you want to make multiple batches of an air fried recipe, start checking the second batch for doneness a few minutes early. This is because the air fryer will already be hot and may cook the second batch more quickly.

Do I need any extras or attachments for my air fryer?

Some air fryers come with attachments, such as racks and pans. While these might be useful for specific purposes, the recipes in Air Fryer Perfection were crafted to use only the basic air-fryer basket. No additional accessories necessary.

How do I prevent food from sticking to my air fryer?

For foods that are prone to sticking, such as breaded chicken or delicate fish, we recommend spraying the basket lightly with vegetable oil spray. You can also use a foil sling to make cleanup and the removal of certain foods easier, especially fish.

How do I clean my air fryer?

To clean your air fryer, start by removing any removable parts, such as the drawer and basket, and washing them in the dishwasher. Consult your air-fryer manual to make sure all parts are dishwasher-safe before proceeding.

Next, clean the main body of your air fryer. Grease and food splatters can build up around the heating element and cause smoking, so it's important to clean this area occasionally. To clean the heating element, turn your air fryer upside down. This will make it easier to access the element and clean it properly.

What do if smell smoke while air frying?

If you encounter smoke or an unpleasant smell while cooking with your air fryer, the first thing you should do is check to see if it needs to be cleaned. If there is excessive smoke or the smell of burning, even when the food isn't burnt, it's likely that there is built-up residue around the heating element. To clean this area, simply remove any food splatter and use mild detergent. Periodically check and clean your air fryer to avoid these issues in the future.

Are air fryers safe to use?

Yes, air fryers are safe to use and are not toxic. Air fryers have lower levels of acrylamide, making them a healthier option than deep-fat frying your food. However, it's important to remember that air fryers are only as healthy as the food you cook in them. So if you're using an air fryer to cook unhealthy foods, they will still be unhealthy.

4-Week Diet Plan

Week 1

Day 1:
Breakfast: Butter Bread
Lunch: Buttered Peas
Snack: Homemade Sausage Rolls
Dinner: Golden Cajun Fish Fillets
Dessert: Easy Apple Crumble

Day 2:
Breakfast: Traditional Scottish Porridge
Lunch: Cheese Cauliflower
Snack: Prawns with Spicy Sauce
Dinner: Honey Roast Duck with Thyme
Dessert: Quick and Easy Banoffee Pie

Day 3:
Breakfast: Homemade Crumpets
Lunch: Thyme Parsnip Soup
Snack: Creamy Leek & Potato Soup with Bread
Dinner: Cheese Turkey Ciabatta
Dessert: Bread and Raisin Pudding

Day 4:
Breakfast: Traditional English Breakfast
Lunch: Traditional Rumbled Thumps
Snack: Yellow Split Pea Ham Soup
Dinner: Simple Fish Fillets
Dessert: Cherry Tart

Day 5:
Breakfast: Grilled Haddock
Lunch: Cheese Leek Sausages
Snack: Classic Welsh Rarebit
Dinner: Easy Fried Duck Breast
Dessert: Classic Yorkshire Curd Tart

Day 6:
Breakfast: Tasty Potato Scone
Lunch: Tasty Scottish Stovies
Snack: Bacon-Wrapped Chicken
Dinner: Herb Roast Beef
Dessert: Lemon Spotted Dick

Day 7:
Breakfast: Potato Bread Farls
Lunch: Vegan Shepherd's Pie
Snack: Easy Yorkshire Pudding
Dinner: Buttered Herb Turkey Breast
Dessert: Homemade Welsh Cakes

Week 2

Day 1:
Breakfast: Apple Ravioli
Lunch: Cheese and Leek tart
Snack: Traditional Bubble and Squeak
Dinner: Crispy Potato-Crusted Fish
Dessert: Apple Cake

Day 2:
Breakfast: Easy Soda Bread
Lunch: Cheese Fennel and Mushrooms Tartlets
Snack: Scottish Cullen Skink
Dinner: Herb-Roasted Lamb
Dessert: Scottish Dundee Cake

Day 3:
Breakfast: Rice with Eggs and Tofu
Lunch: Thyme Pumpkin Soup
Snack: Air fryer Sausage and Chips
Dinner: Turkey Strips with Three Peppers
Dessert: Easy Peach Cobbler

Day 4:
Breakfast: Scottish Short Bread Cookies
Lunch: All-Vegetable Toad in The Hole
Snack: Delicious Beef Wellington Bites
Dinner: Simple Air Fryer Sausages
Dessert: Rhubarb Muffins with Oats Crumble

Day 5:
Breakfast: Simple Poached Eggs on Toast
Lunch: Pea and Mint Soup with Ham
Snack: Mushroom and Prosciutto on Toast
Dinner: Pork Cassoulet with Beans and Carrots
Dessert: Victoria Sponge Cake

Day 6:
Breakfast: Classic Eggs Benedict
Lunch: Cheese Potato & Lentil Pie
Snack: Potted Prawns with Bread
Dinner: Spicy Turkey Wings
Dessert: Baked Manchester Tart

Day 7:
Breakfast: Scrambled Eggs with Smoked Salmon
Lunch: Herby Veggie Balls
Snack: Pineapple Sticks with Yogurt Dip
Dinner: Beer Battered Cod
Dessert: Oat Flapjacks

Week 3

Day 1:
Breakfast: Hot Cross Buns
Lunch: Vegetarian Cheese Bean Patties
Snack: Air fry Brussels Sprouts with Bacon
Dinner: Herbed Turkey Crown
Dessert: Custard Tart with Nutmeg

Day 2:
Breakfast: Tuscan Bean Tomato Toast
Lunch: Roasted Potatoes
Snack: Air fryer Sausage and Chips
Dinner: Spicy Lemon Fish
Dessert: Apple Cake with Walnut

Day 3:
Breakfast: Strawberry Jam On toast
Lunch: Cheese Cauliflower
Snack: Crispy Fish and Chips
Dinner: Air Fryer Garlic Prawns
Dessert: Simple Apple Pie

Day 4:
Breakfast: Baked Eggs and Salmon
Lunch: Buttered Peas
Snack: Cockle Pie
Dinner: Roast Lamb Legs with Potatoes
Dessert: Homemade Sweet Potato Pie

Day 5:
Breakfast: Bacon Butty Sandwich
Lunch: Thyme Parsnip Soup
Snack: Grilled Leeks in Cheese Milk Sauce
Dinner: Spicy Turkey Tenderloin
Dessert: Mini Cinnamon Apple Pie

Day 6:
Breakfast: Almond Tarts with Cherry Jam
Lunch: Traditional Rumbled Thumps
Snack: Fish Cakes
Dinner: Air Fryer Beef Hamburgers
Dessert: Easy Apple Crumble

Day 7:
Breakfast: Rhubarb, Pear and Hazelnut Crumble
Lunch: Cheese Leek Sausages
Snack: Delicious Beef Wellington Bites
Dinner: Finnan Haddie
Dessert: Quick and Easy Banoffee Pie

Week 4

Day 1:
Breakfast: Butter Bread
Lunch: Tasty Scottish Stovies
Snack: Halloumi Corn Bites
Dinner: Breaded Chicken Breast
Dessert: Bread and Raisin Pudding

Day 2:
Breakfast: Traditional Scottish Porridge
Lunch: Vegan Shepherd's Pie
Snack: Golden Beef Pies
Dinner: Potted Butter Scallops
Dessert: Cherry Tart

Day 3:
Breakfast: Homemade Crumpets
Lunch: Cheese and Leek tart
Snack: Homemade Sausage Rolls
Dinner: Easy Fried Chicken Legs
Dessert: Classic Yorkshire Curd Tart

Day 4:
Breakfast: Traditional English Breakfast
Lunch: Cheese Fennel and Mushrooms Tartlets
Snack: Prawns with Spicy Sauce
Dinner: Beef, Vegetables with Noodles
Dessert: Lemon Spotted Dick

Day 5:
Breakfast: Grilled Haddock
Lunch: Thyme Pumpkin Soup
Snack: Creamy Leek & Potato Soup with Bread
Dinner: Easy Roast Steak
Dessert: Homemade Welsh Cakes

Day 6:
Breakfast: Tasty Potato Scone
Lunch: All-Vegetable Toad in The Hole
Snack: Yellow Split Pea Ham Soup
Dinner: Italian Seasoned Chicken
Dessert: Apple Cake

Day 7:
Breakfast: Potato Bread Farl
Lunch: Pea and Mint Soup with Ham
Snack: Classic Welsh Rarebit
Dinner: Bacon-Wrapped Oyster
Dessert: Scottish Dundee Cake

Chapter 1 Breakfast Recipes

Butter Bread

Prep Time: 40 minutes | Cooking Time: 20 minutes | Servings: 6

Ingredients:

250g bread flour
115g butter
1¼ teaspoons dried yeast

2 tablespoons caster sugar
1 pinch of salt
240ml warm water

Extra flour for kneading and rolling

Preparation:

1. Mix yeast with water and sugar and set aside till the yeast activates. 2. Knead flour and salt by slowly adding the yeast mixture. If the mixture is too sticky add more flour. 3. Knead into a smooth dough and let it rest for 30 minutes. 4. When doubles in size knead the dough again for one minute, roll it with the rolling pin until its ½ cm thick. 5. Smear the butter and roll the fold the dough into a rectangle. Cut small rectangles. Cover them for 10 minutes. 6. Preheat Air fryer to 200°C for 20 minutes. 7. Place parchment paper in the Air fryer basket. Place butteries in the basket in a single layer. 8. Cook for 20 minutes. Remove and cook the other batch. 9. Serve right away.

Serving Suggestions: Serve with vanilla cream and icing sugar.
Variation Tip: you can use self-rising flour instead of bread flour.
Nutritional Information per Serving:
Calories: 305 | Fat: 15.8g | Sat Fat: 9.8g | Carbohydrates: 36g | Fibre: 1.3g | Sugar: 4.1g | Protein: 4.8g

Traditional Scottish Porridge

Prep Time: 5 minutes | Cooking Time: 5 minutes | Servings: 2

Ingredients:

40g rolled oats

240ml whole milk

Pinch of salt

Preparation:

1. Preheat air fryer at 95°C. 2. In a small bowl that fits the air fryer basket, add oats and the rest of the ingredients. 3. Mix and put in the air fryer for 3 minutes. Stir and change the side of the bowl and cook again for 2 more minutes. 4. Serve warm.

Serving Suggestions: You can serve with bananas, pecans and walnuts.
Variation Tip: You can use plant based milk instead of whole milk.
Nutritional Information per Serving:
Calories: 301 | Fat: 10.6g | Sat Fat: 5g | Carbohydrates: 38.7g | Fibre: 4.1g | Sugar: 13.2g | Protein: 13.2g

Homemade Crumpets

Prep Time: 5 minutes | Cooking Time: 18 minutes | Servings: 2

Ingredients:

125g plain flour
180ml warm water
½ teaspoon salt

½ teaspoon white sugar
1 teaspoon baking powder
1 teaspoon yeast

1 tablespoon warm water
2 tablespoons unsalted melted butter

Preparation:

1. Mix flour, baking powder and salt in a mixing bowl. 2. Put yeast in the warm water along with sugar. Add this mixture in the flour when it puffs up. 3. Mix flour lightly with the hand mixer or an electric mixer. 4. Cover the mixture with the cling wrap and let it rest until it rises. 5. Grease the 15 cm foil cups with the butter and pour ¼ cup of the mixture in the cups. 6. Line the cups in the air fryer basket in a single layer. 7. Cook for 6 minutes at 200°C. 8. Remove crumpets and cook others in batches.

Serving Suggestions: Serve with icing sugar or raspberry jam.
Variation Tip: You can also top with butter for variations.
Nutritional Information per Serving:
Calories: 167 | Fat: 5.8g | Sat Fat: 3.7g | Carbohydrates: 24.5g | Fibre: 1.2g | Sugar: 1.5g | Protein: 3.4g

Traditional English Breakfast

Prep Time: 5 minutes | Cooking Time: 10 minutes | Servings: 4

Ingredients:

2 large eggs
Salt & pepper
6 English sausages

4 large mushrooms
1 teaspoon butter
6 bacon

2 large tomatoes
½ can baked beans

Preparation:

1. Grease two ramekins with butter and crack eggs. 2. Place the ramekins in the air fryer basket along with bacon, sausages, tomatoes and mushrooms. 3. Season mushrooms and tomatoes with salt and pepper. 4. Cook for 5 minutes in 180°C. Remove eggs from the air fryer. Cook the rest for another 5 minutes. 5. Dish out and serve warm with canned beans.
Serving Suggestions: Serve with toast and English tea.
Variation Tip: You can also do scrambled eggs.
Nutritional Information per Serving:
Calories: 149 | Fat: 124g | Sat Fat: 42g | Carbohydrates: 22 g | Fibre: 6g | Sugar: 4g | Protein: 70g

Grilled Haddock

Prep Time: 5 minutes | Cooking Time: 15 minutes | Servings: 6

Ingredients:

900g smoked haddock fillets
480ml warm milk

2 tablespoons flour
55g melted butter

Preparation:

1. Preheat Air fryer at 175°C for 15 minutes. 2. Mix flour, milk and butter until smooth. 3. Add fish in an air fryer deep dish. Pour milk mixture. 4. Set the function to Grill and place the Baking Pan in the air fryer. Cook for 15 minutes. 5. Dish out and serve.
Serving Suggestions: Serve with lime.
Variation Tip: You can also serve with cooked peas.
Nutritional Information per Serving:
Calories: 294 | Fat: 11g | Sat Fat: 6g | Carbohydrates:6g | Fibre: 0g | Sugar: 4g | Protein: 41g

Tasty Potato Scone

Prep Time: 20 minutes | Cooking Time: 15 minutes | Servings: 4

Ingredients:

125g flour
½ tablespoons baking powder
115g mashed potatoes

3 tablespoons milk
½ teaspoon salt
1½ tablespoons butter

1 large egg

Preparation:

1. In a mixing bowl, mix all the dry ingredients. 2. Cut butter into pieces in the flour mixture and mix until it is crumbly. 3. Then add rest of the wet ingredients and knead well until the dough is soft and smooth. Add a tablespoon of flour if the dough is sticky. 4. Roll the dough into a log and cut 2.5cm circles. 5. Preheat the air fryer at 175°C. 6. Grease the air fryer basket and place the scones. Cook for 14 minutes flipping half way through to the cook time. 7. Dish out and serve.
Serving Suggestions: Serve with butter.
Variation Tip: You can make mashed potatoes with butter and milk to make the scones softer.
Nutritional Information per Serving:
Calories: 199 | Fat: 6g | Sat Fat: 3g | Carbohydrates: 30g | Fibre: 1g | Sugar: 1g | Protein: 6g

Potato Bread Farls

Prep Time: 20 minutes | Cooking Time: 15 minutes | Servings: 4

Ingredients:

4 medium sized boiled potatoes
30g flour

1 pinch salt
1 tablespoon melted butter

Preparation:

1. Mash boiled potatoes. 2. Dump rest of the ingredients in the potatoes and mix until it forms a dough 3. Roll out the dough with the rolling pin until ½ cm thick. Cut into quarters. 4. Preheat air fryer at 185°C. Line the basket with the parchment paper and place the quarters in a single layer. 5. Air fry for 15 minutes flipping in between the cook time. 6. Serve warm.
Serving Suggestions: You can serve with eggs and butter
Variation Tip: You can also use ground pepper for some taste variation.
Nutritional Information per Serving:
Calories: 201 | Fat: 3.2g | Sat Fat: 1.9g | Carbohydrates: 39.4g | Fibre: 5.3g | Sugar: 2.5g | Protein: 4.4g

Apple Ravioli

Prep Time: 10 minutes | Cooking Time: 18 minutes | Servings: 3

Ingredients:

Filling
1 medium size apple
1-2 tablespoons water

¼ teaspoon cinnamon
Pinch of salt

Dough
90g flour
2 medium size boiled and finely mashed potatoes

½ teaspoon sugar
1 tablespoon softened unsalted butter
¼ teaspoon salt

Oil for spraying

Preparation:

1. For Filling: Finely grate apples and heat them with some water, cinnamon and salt. Cook until they are soft and mushy. In the end add sugar and mix until sugar is dissolved completely and all the moisture evaporates. Let it cool completely. 2. For Dough: Mix mashed potatoes with the rest of the ingredients. Knead until a smooth dough is formed. Let it rest for 10 minutes. 3. Preheat Air fryer at 175°C for 10 minutes. Line the air fryer basket with the parchment paper. 4. Divide the dough in 12 balls and flatten out each ball with the rolling pin until it is 1cm thick. 5. Next add the apple filling on one side and cover it with the other side to form a semi-circle. 6. Spray or brush oil on both sides and place the bread in the air fryer basket in a single layer 7. Cook it for 10 minutes, flipping it half way through the cooking time. 8. Repeat the same steps for the next batches. 9. Dish out, cut in quarters and serve immediately.
Serving Suggestions: Serve garnished with your favourite greens and pomegranate seeds.
Variation Tip: You can skip cinnamon for taste variation.
Nutritional Information per Serving:
Calories: 158 | Fat: 6.4g | Sat Fat: 2.2g | Carbohydrates: 30.1g | Fibre: 2.9g | Sugar: 5.2g | Protein: 3.6g

Easy Soda Bread

Prep Time: 8 minutes | Cooking Time: 10 minutes | Servings: 4

Ingredients:

250g plain flour, plus extra for dusting
1 teaspoon sugar

1 teaspoon bicarbonate of soda
½ teaspoon salt

240ml buttermilk

Preparation:

1. Sift the Flour with sugar, salt and soda bi carbonate. 2. Add buttermilk in the dry ingredients and knead until a dough is formed. 3. Roll out the dough on the floured surface and cut into your desired shapes. 4. Preheat Air fryer on 200°C for 10 minutes. 5. Place baking paper in the basket and place soda bread in a single layer. 6. Cook for 10 minutes, flipping half way through to the cook time. 7. Dish out, split it open and serve warm with butter.
Serving Suggestions: Serve with traditional English tea.
Variation Tip: You can also dust with icing sugar or top with honey.
Nutritional Information per Serving:
Calories: 248 | Fat: 0.5g | Sat Fat: 0.3g | Carbohydrates: 49.9g | Fibre: 2g | Sugar: 5.9g | Protein: 8g

Rice with Eggs and Tofu

Prep Time: 10 minutes | Cooking Time: 20 minutes | Servings: 4

Ingredients:

120ml milk
225g smoked tofu
1 onion, finely chopped
1 tablespoon olive oil
½ teaspoon crushed garlic

½ teaspoon ginger, chopped
½ teaspoon ground turmeric
1 tablespoon medium curry powder
½ teaspoon ground coriander
400g long grain rice

360ml vegetable stock
2 tablespoons fresh parsley, roughly chopped
4 eggs

Preparation:

1. Place the eggs in the air fryer basket and let them cook for 10 min on 145°C. Once cooked, remove them from the air fryer and put them in the ice water for 5 minutes. Peel them and cut them in quarters. Set aside. 2. Bring a boil to water and milk in a saucepan over medium saucepan. Place tofu and poach for 5 minutes. Turn off the heat and set it aside. 3. In another pan sauté onion in olive oil. Add ginger, garlic, turmeric and curry powder. Cook till onions are translucent. 4. Add vegetable stock and rice. cover and cook on low heat for 10-12 minutes. 5. Remove tofu from the liquid and shred in small pieces. Add the remaining poaching liquid in the rice and cook for 5 minutes with the lid on. 6. When rice is done stir the tofu in and dish out. 7. Top with parsley and quartered eggs. serve warm.

Serving Suggestions: Serve with sour cream or yogurt.
Variation Tip: You can also use almond or coconut milk for poaching Haddock.
Nutritional Information per Serving:
Calories: 461 | Fat: 12g | Sat Fat: 3g | Carbohydrates: 61.3g | Fibre: 1.8g | Sugar: 6g | Protein: 32.6g

Scottish Short Bread Cookies

Prep Time: 15 minutes | Cooking Time: 10 minutes | Servings: 8

Ingredients:

500g flour

205g brown sugar

460g softened butter

Preparation:

1. Preheat Air fryer at 145°C for 10 minutes. 2. In a stand mixer cream together butter and sugar. Add flour slowly to the mixture and mix until a smooth dough is formed. 3. Place the dough on a lightly floured surface and roll out with the rolling pin till it is 1 cm thick. Cut out 3x2.5cm long cookies and prick with the fork. 4. Place cookies in the basket 2.5cm apart in a single layer and cook for 7-9 minutes. 5. Remove from the air fryer once it is lightly brown and crisp. 6. Cook the remaining batches repeating the same steps. 7. Serve immediately.

Serving Suggestions: Serve with earl gray tea.
Variation Tip: Add light brown sugar instead of dark brown sugar.
Nutritional Information per Serving:
Calories: 381 | Fat: 16.7g | Sat Fat: 10.4g | Carbohydrates: 52.4g | Fibre: 1.4g | Sugar: 14.2g | Protein: 5.4g

Simple Poached Eggs on Toast

Prep Time: 5 minutes | Cooking Time: 10 minutes | Servings: 2

Ingredients:

2 eggs
2 slices bread

Salt and pepper for seasoning
Oil for spraying

Preparation:

1. Preheat Air fryer at 180°C for 10 minutes. 2. Grease ramekins with oil and crack egg in each. Add 2 tablespoons of water and place in the air fryer basket. Cook for 4 minutes. 3. Remove ramekins and place toast in the basket. Cook for 4 minutes and remove from the air fryer once it is lightly brown and crisp. 4. Put eggs on toast and sprinkle with salt and pepper. 5. Serve immediately.

Serving Suggestions: Serve with coffee.
Variation Tip: You can top it with parsley as well.
Nutritional Information per Serving:
Calories: 147 | Fat: 11.5g | Sat Fat: 2.3g | Carbohydrates: 4.9g | Fibre: 0.2g | Sugar: 0.7g | Protein: 6.2g

Classic Eggs Benedict

Prep Time: 15 minutes | Cooking Time: 12 minutes | Servings: 4

Ingredients:

4 large egg yolks at room temperature
115g unsalted butter, melted
1½ tablespoons freshly squeezed lemon juice

Pinch of salt and pepper
Pinch of cayenne pepper
2 English muffins
4 large eggs

8 tablespoons water
4 slices bacon
Fresh chives, chopped

Preparation:

1. Preheat Air fryer at 200°C for 10 minutes. 2. For Sauce: Blend together yolks, lemon juice, salt and pepper until it turns light yellow in color. Blend again by slowly drizzling the melted butter until fully incorporated. Keep the sauce aside. 3. Cut English muffins in halves and place in the air fryer basket. Cook for 4 minutes and remove from the air fryer once it is lightly brown and crisp. 4. Next place the bacon in the basket and cook for 2 minutes until cooked. 5. Crack eggs in 4 ramekins. Add 2 tablespoons of water in each ramekin. Set the temperature of the air fryer to 180°C and place the ramekins in the basket. Cook the eggs and then remove from the air fryer. 6. Assembling: Place the bacon on top of each English muffin adding eggs on top of each. Generously drizzle the sauce over each tower. 7. Garnish with cayenne pepper and chopped chives on top. 8. Serve immediately.

Serving Suggestions: Serve with your favorite greens and grilled tomatoes.
Variation Tip: You can skip Cayenne pepper.
Nutritional Information per Serving:
Calories: 448 | Fat: 35g | Sat Fat: 18g | Carbohydrates: 15g | Fibre: 1g | Sugar: 1g | Protein: 20g

Hot Cross Buns

Prep Time: 60 minutes | Cooking Time: 16 minutes | Servings: 12

Ingredients:

440g flour
3 large eggs room temperature
70g raisins
¾ tablespoons dry instant yeast

100g granulated sugar and ½ teaspoon
180ml warm milk
4 tablespoons butter unsalted & room temperature

½ teaspoon salt
¼ teaspoon ground clove
¼ teaspoon ground nutmeg
¼ teaspoon ground cinnamon

For Glaze:
60g icing sugar

1½ teaspoons milk

1 teaspoon orange or lemon juice

Preparation:

1. Preheat Air fryer at 115°C for 10 minutes. 2. In a bowl add warm milk, yeast and ½ teaspoon sugar. Set it aside till the mixture turns frothy. 3. In a stand mixture cream together remaining sugar, butter and two eggs. 4. Add sifted flour to the butter mixture along with salt, cinnamon, nutmeg and clove. 5. Add yeast mixture and knead until a smooth dough is formed. 6. Mix raisins and knead again. Keep the dough in a greased pan for 40 minutes until the dough rises. 7. When the dough doubles in size, take it out on a floured surface, knead a little and divide into 12 balls. Let the balls sit for 10 minutes until they rise a bit. 8. Prepare Egg wash: Whisk the remaining one egg with 2 tablespoons of water to make an egg wash. 9. Line the balls in the air fryer basket in a single layer and cook for 16 minutes. After 5 min brush the buns with egg wash and cook for 10 more minutes. 10. Remove the buns and let them cook. Repeat the same steps for the next batch. 11. Glaze: Mix all the ingredients of the glaze and fill in the piping bag. 12. Once the buns are cool, pipe the glaze in the form of crosses on top of the buns. 13. Serve immediately.

Serving Suggestions: Serve with butter.
Variation Tip: You can add cranberries instead of raisins.
Nutritional Information per Serving:
Calories: 234 | Fat: 2g | Sat Fat: 1g | Carbohydrates: 47g | Fibre: 2g | Sugar: 14g | Protein: 6g

Tuscan Bean Tomato Toast

Prep Time: 15 minutes | Cooking Time: 10 minutes | Servings: 2

Ingredients:

2 slices of sourdough bread
2 tablespoons olive oil, plus 2 tsp for
drizzling

1 chopped red onion
1 garlic clove, crushed
salt and freshly ground black pepper

1 can of chunky tomatoes
1 tin of haricot beans
1 sprig fresh rosemary

Preparation:

1. Preheat Air fryer at 175°C for 10 minutes. 2. Drizzle oil on the bread slices and toast on in the air fryer for 4 minutes until lightly brown and crisp. 3. In a skillet heat olive oil and sauté onion until translucent. Add garlic and tomatoes and cook for 2 minutes. 4. Add beans and rosemary along with salt and pepper. Simmer for 8 minutes. 5. Place beans on top of the toast and serve immediately.

Serving Suggestions: Serve with grated parmesan and chopped chili on top.

Variation Tip: You can use any beans.

Nutritional Information per Serving:

Calories: 478 | Fat: 16.5g | Sat Fat: 2g | Carbohydrates: 60g | Fibre: 12.5g | Sugar: 11.5g | Protein: 17g

Strawberry Jam On toast

Prep Time: 2 minutes | Cooking Time: 4 minutes | Servings: 2

Ingredients:

1 teaspoon butter

2 slices of whole wheat bread

Strawberry Jam

Preparation:

1. Preheat Air fryer at 145°C for 4 minutes. 2. Smear butter on the bread slices and place them in the air fryer basket. Cook for 2 minutes and then turn the sides. Cook for another 2 minutes. Remove from the air fryer once it is lightly brown and crisp. 3. Smear jam on the slices and serve immediately.

Serving Suggestions: Serve with English tea.

Variation Tip: You can use preserves instead of jam as well.

Nutritional Information per Serving:

Calories: 381 | Fat: 16.7g | Sat Fat: 10.4g | Carbohydrates: 52.4g | Fibre: 1.4g | Sugar: 14.2g | Protein: 5.4g

Baked Eggs and Salmon

Prep Time: 5 minutes | Cooking Time: 5 minutes | Servings: 2

Ingredients:

2 eggs at room temperature
2 slices of smoked salmon

Handful of mushrooms
1 teaspoons of chopped chives

Salt and ground black pepper for seasoning.
Oil for spraying

Preparation:

1. Preheat Air fryer at 150°C for 5 minutes. 2. Grease a bowl or ramekin with the oil. Add mushrooms and chopped smoked salmon. Crack an egg on top. Sprinkle with salt and black pepper. 3. Place the bowls in the air fryer basket and cook for 5 minutes. 4. Garnish with chopped chives. 5. Serve immediately.

Serving Suggestions: Serve with English muffins or bread of your choice.

Variation Tip: Add any other vegetables or black pudding for taste variation.

Nutritional Information per Serving:

Calories: 77 | Fat: 3.6g | Sat Fat: 0.6g | Carbohydrates: 1.6g | Fibre: 0.6g | Sugar: 0.7g | Protein: 9.3g

Almond Tarts with Cherry Jam

Prep Time: 20 minutes | Cooking Time: 18 minutes | Servings: 12

Ingredients:

1 pack of 375g ready to cook puff pastry
80g morello cherry jam
115g softened butter
70g caster sugar

2 medium eggs
30g flaked almond
90g self-rising flour
70g ground almond

½ tsp almond extract
60g icing sugar for decoration

Preparation:

1. Preheat Air fryer at 200°C for 18 minutes. 2. Divide the pastry sheet into two and roll out each sheet thinly. Spread jam on it. 3. Cream together butter, sugar, eggs and almond extract. Fold flour and ground almonds in the mixture and spread on the tart on top of jam. 4. Cover the tart with the other half of the sheet. 5. Spread flaked almonds on top. 6. Cover the pan with the foil and put it in the air fryer basket. Cook for 10 minutes. Remove the foil and cook for another 8 minutes. 7. Dust icing sugar on top. 8. Serve immediately.

Serving Suggestions: Serve with cherry sauce.

Variation Tip: you can use almond flour instead of self-rising flour.

Nutritional Information per Serving:

Calories: 362 | Fat: 20g | Sat Fat: 9g | Carbohydrates: 39g | Fibre: 1g | Sugar: 23g | Protein: 6g

Rhubarb, Pear and Hazelnut Crumble

Prep Time: 15 minutes | Cooking Time: 20 minutes | Servings: 4

Ingredients:

For Filling:

2 ripe pears (cubed)
240g diced rhubarb
2 teaspoons lemon zest

1 tablespoon lemon juice
50g caster sugar
1 teaspoon vanilla extract

115g cold butter (cut in cubes)

For Crumble:

60g toasted hazelnuts (chopped)
180g flour

50g caster sugar
¼ teaspoon sea salt

Preparation:

1. Preheat Air fryer at 200°C for 10 minutes. 2. In a heavy bottomed pan, cook the ingredients of filling except the butter until the moisture is evaporated and pear and rhubarb is soft. 3. In another bowl mix the ingredients of filling with butter and mix with hand until there is a crumbly texture. 4. In a dish pour filling and spread crumble mixture on top. 5. Place the dish in the air fryer basket and let it cook for 20 minutes. 6. Serve immediately.

Serving Suggestions: Serve with vanilla yogurt or ice cream

Variation Tip: You can replace caster sugar with brown sugar.

Nutritional Information per Serving:

Calories: 446 | Fat: 27.4g | Sat Fat: 11.8g | Carbohydrates: 49.6g | Fibre: 5.6g | Sugar: 29.1g | Protein: 5.1g

Scrambled Eggs with Smoked Salmon

Prep Time: 10 minutes | Cooking Time: 16 minutes | Servings: 4

Ingredients:

115g sliced smoked salmon

6 eggs

1 tablespoons butter

60g heavy cream

Salt and freshly ground black pepper

2 tablespoons finely chopped fresh chives.

4 English Muffins

Preparation:

1. Preheat Air fryer at 175°C for 6 minutes. 2. Cut English muffins in half and place them in the air fryer for 6 minutes until crisp. Remove on the plate. 3. Slice salmon into pieces. Reserve two slices of salmon and cut the rest in small pieces. 4. Whisk eggs and cream together until fully combined. Season with salt and pepper. Add one tablespoon of chopped chives and mix well. 5. Grease a bowl with butter and pour the batter in that bowl. Place it in the air fryer. Air fry eggs for 10 minutes at 175°C. Stir after 5 min and add salmon pieces. Mix with a fork and cook for another 5 min. 6. Place the eggs on the muffins and garnish with reserved salmon pieces and chives. 7. Serve immediately.

Serving Suggestions: Serve with coffee

Variation Tip: You can replace cream with milk.

Nutritional Information per Serving:

Calories: 309 | Fat: 14.4g | Sat Fat: 6.3g | Carbohydrates: 26.1g | Fibre: 2.1g | Sugar: 2.6g | Protein: 18.8g

Bacon Butty Sandwich

Prep Time: 5 minutes | Cooking Time: 7 minutes | Servings: 1

Ingredients:

2 slices bacon

2 slices of farmhouse bread

½ teaspoon butter

¼ teaspoon HP steak sauce

¼ teaspoon Worcestershire sauce

Preparation:

1. Preheat Air fryer at 175°C for 7 minutes. 2. Place bacon strips in the basket and cook for 4 minutes. Once done, remove from the air fryer. 3. Next place bread slices in the air fryer in a single layer and cook for 3 minutes. 4. Remove from the air fryer once it is lightly brown and crisp. 5. Assemble Bacon Butty by smearing butter on the slices. Next place bacon strips and drizzle Hp sauce and Worcestershire sauce. Place the other slice on top. 6. Serve immediately.

Serving Suggestions: Serve with favorite dipping sauce.

Variation Tip: You can use turkey bacon.

Nutritional Information per Serving:

Calories: 169 | Fat: 6.4g | Sat Fat: 2.2g | Carbohydrates: 22.9g | Fibre: 1.3g | Sugar: 4.3g | Protein: 5.1g

Chapter 2 Snack and Starter Recipes

Homemade Sausage Rolls

Prep Time: 25 minutes | Cooking Time: 14 minutes | Servings: 6 - 10

Ingredients:

625g puff pastry
900g sausage meat
3 medium eggs (divided)

1 tablespoon vegetable oil
1 medium onion (chopped)
Ground black pepper, to taste

Salt, to taste

Preparation:

1. Preheat air fryer at 95°C for 14 minutes 2. In a pan, heat oil and saute onions until translucent. 3. In a mixing bowl, add sausage meat, 2 eggs, sauté onions and season them with salt and pepper. 4. Unroll the puff pastry and cut in 10 cm strips. Place sausage meat mixture in the center in the form of a line. Fold the puff pastry on the sausage meat and seal the corners. cut the rolls in 5cm size. 5. Beat one egg in a small bowl and brush egg wash on the rolls. 6. Place rolls in the air fryer basket in a single layer. Cook for 12-14 minutes until golden and crisp. 7. Dish out and serve warm.
Serving Suggestions: Serve with ketchup.
Variation Tip: You can also use sage and thyme to season the sausage meat.
Nutritional Information per Serving:
Calories: 717 | Fat: 56g | Sat Fat: 13g | Carbohydrates: 36g | Fibre: 1g | Sugar: 2g | Protein: 18g

Prawns with Spicy Sauce

Prep Time: 5 minutes | Cooking Time: 8 minutes | Servings: 6

Ingredients:

Sauce:
120g chili sauce
1 teaspoon hot sauce

120g ketchup
3 tablespoon Horseradish

Juice of half lemon

Prawns:
900g prawns, clean and deveined

1 tsp salt

1 tsp black pepper

Preparation:

1. For sauce: Mix all the ingredients and pour in a bowl. 2. Prepare Prawns: Place prawns in the air fry basket in a single layer. Season with salt and pepper 3. Air fry for 5-8 minutes at 200°C. Flip once through half of the cooking time. 4. Dish out and serve with the sauce.
Serving Suggestions: Garnish with dill leaves.
Variation Tip: You can also marinate prawns with lemon.
Nutritional Information per Serving:
Calories: 117 | Fat: 43g | Sat Fat: 13g | Carbohydrates: 54g | Fibre: 1g | Sugar: 2g | Protein: 32g

Creamy Leek & Potato Soup with Bread

Prep Time: 20 minutes | Cooking Time: 16 minutes | Servings: 6

Ingredients:

5 medium-sized potatoes (peeled and diced)
350g of leeks (white part)
960ml of chicken stock

120g heavy cream
120ml milk
1 small onion finely chopped

Salt and pepper for seasoning
3½ tablespoons of butter
One slice of bread.

Preparation:

1. Preheat air fryer at 200°C. 2. In a large pan, heat butter and add potatoes and leeks with onions. 3. Add salt and pepper along with the stock. Cover and let it simmer for 10 minutes. 4. Cut the bread into small pieces and spray it with oil. Position them in the Air fryer basket. Air fry for 6 minutes until golden and crisp. 5. Once the vegetables are cooked, puree this in a blender until smooth. 6. Dump the puree again in the pot and mix cream and milk. Adjust the seasoning. 7. Dish out and serve with bread and chopped leek.
Serving Suggestions: You can drizzle some heavy cream on top.
Variation Tip: To make it healthier, you can replace cream and full fat milk with low fat milk.
Nutritional Information per Serving:
Calories: 252 | Fat: 18g | Sat Fat: 11g | Carbohydrates: 18g | Fibre: 3g | Sugar: 0g | Protein: 5g

Yellow Split Pea Ham Soup

Prep Time: 30 minutes | Cooking Time: 35 minutes | Servings: 6

Ingredients:

150g yellow split peas
135g pulled ham hocks
1 large carrot - diced
5 baby potatoes cubed

780ml water
1 tablespoon olive oil
2 cloves garlic, minced
½ medium onion, peeled and diced

¼ teaspoon salt
¼ teaspoon ground black pepper

Preparation:

1. Place a large skillet with oil on medium heat. 2. Add onions and garlic, stir cook for 1 minute then add potatoes and carrots along with salt and pepper. 3. Stir cook for 5 minutes then add water, yellow split pea and half of the ham. 4. Cover and slow cook for another 30 minutes. 5. Once the soup is done, puree it using stick blender coarsely. 6. Place the remaining pulled ham in the air fry basket. Spray oil and let it air fry for 4 minutes on 40°C. 7. Dish out the soup and top it with the crisp ham.

Serving Suggestions: Serve with your favourite bread.

Variation Tip: you can use your favourite seasoning in the soup for taste variation.

Nutritional Information per Serving:

Calories: 239 | Fat: 3.2g | Sat Fat: 0.6g | Carbohydrates: 43.9g | Fibre: 11.4g | Sugar: 6.1g | Protein: 14g

Classic Welsh Rarebit

Prep Time: 5 minutes | Cooking Time: 10 minutes | Servings: 6

Ingredients:

12 thick slices white bread
1 large egg, lightly beaten
100g grated cheddar cheese

2 tablespoons whole milk
1 teaspoon English mustard
1 teaspoons Worcestershire sauce

Pinch cayenne pepper

Preparation:

1. Set the temperature to 175°C and preheat for 10 minutes. 2. Set aside one tablespoon of cheese. Combine the rest with egg, milk, Worcestershire sauce, mustard and cayenne pepper. 3. Place the cheese mixture on the bread slices and sprinkle reserved cheese on top of them. 4. Place the bread in a single layer in the air fryer basket. Air fry for 10 minutes until the cheese is melted. 5. Dish out and serve.

Serving Suggestions: Serve with marinara sauce and fresh parsley.

Variation Tip: You can replace cayenne pepper with paprika to enhance the taste.

Nutritional Information per Serving:

Calories: 162 | Fat: 23g | Sat Fat: 13g | Carbohydrates: 26.8g | Fibre: 1.4g | Sugar: 2g | Protein: 21.2g

Bacon-Wrapped Chicken

Prep Time: 5 minutes | Cooking Time: 12 minutes | Servings: 10

Ingredients:

675g boneless chicken breast, cut in 2.5cm chunks

10 slices bacon

Preparation:

1. Wrap the bacon around chicken pieces and stick in a toothpick to seal. 2. Place the wrapped chicken in the Baking Pan. 3. Preheat the air fryer at 200°C for 12 minutes. 4. Place the pieces in a single layer in the air fryer basket and cook for 12 minutes. 5. Flip the pieces once cooked halfway through. 6. Dish out and serve after inserting toothpicks into each.

Serving Suggestions: You can serve with Thai sweet chili sauce.

Variation Tip: You can serve with tartar sauce too.

Nutritional Information per Serving:

Calories: 337 | Fat: 19.8g | Sat Fat: 1.4g | Carbohydrates: 5.1g | Fibre: 0.9g | Sugar: 1.4g | Protein: 37.8g

Easy Yorkshire Pudding

Prep Time: 5 minutes | Cooking Time: 15 minutes | Servings: 4

Ingredients:

1 tablespoon extra-virgin olive oil
65g plain flour

1 small egg
180ml whole milk

Salt & pepper
Oil spray for greasing

Preparation:

1. Preheat Air fryer to 200°C for 15 minutes. 2. Mix plain flour with salt and pepper. Slowly add egg and milk. Whisk thoroughly until the batter becomes thick and bubbles are formed on the surface. 3. Grease Yorkshire pudding tins with oil and place in the air fryer until very hot. 4. Fill the tins halfway through with the batter and place in the air fryer. Cook for 15 minutes.

Serving Suggestions: Serve with sour cream.

Variation Tip: You can also add one more egg white to make the puddings rise more.

Nutritional Information per Serving:

Calories: 115 | Fat: 6g | Sat Fat: 2g | Carbohydrates: 11g | Fibre: 1g | Sugar: 2g | Protein: 4g.

Traditional Bubble and Squeak

Prep Time: 5 minutes | Cooking Time: 12 minutes | Servings: 2

Ingredients:

70g leftover cooked meat
40g cabbage (cut in Julien)

460g leftover mashed potatoes
25g grated cheddar cheese

Salt & pepper
2 tsps thyme

Preparation:

1. In a mixing bowl dump all the ingredients and mix well and put in a heat proof dish that fits in the air fryer. 2. Preheat the air fryer at 180°C for 8 minutes. 3. Place the dish in the air fryer and cook for 8 minutes and then set the temperature at 200°C, cook further for 4 minutes 4. Serve warm.

Serving Suggestions: You can serve it with sour cream.

Variation Tip: You can use any variety of leftovers as per your liking.

Nutritional Information per Serving:

Calories: 359 | Fat: 14.7g | Sat Fat: 5.4g | Carbohydrates: 38.4g | Fibre: 4.4g | Sugar: 4.2g | Protein: 18.4g

Air fryer Sausage and Chips

Prep Time: 2 minutes | Cooking Time: 16 minutes | Servings: 4

Ingredients:

8 frozen sausages

675g frozen chips

Preparation:

1. Preheat Air fryer for 12 minutes at 200°C. 2. Once preheated, spread chips in the basket and place sausages on top of them. Cook for 4 minutes. 3. Toss with the tong and cook again for another 8 minutes. 4. Dish out and serve warm.

Serving Suggestions: Serve with tomato ketchup or chili garlic sauce.

Variation Tip: You can add your favorite seasoning on the chips. Add a dollop of sour cream on top.

Nutritional Information per Serving:

Calories: 240 | Fat: 9.9g | Sat Fat: 2.8g | Carbohydrates: 26.6g | Fibre: 2.1g | Sugar: 2.2g | Protein: 18g

Scottish Cullen Skink

Prep Time: 10 minutes | Cooking Time: 25 minutes | Servings: 4

Ingredients:

2 slices smoked haddock
2 medium potatoes (peeled and cubed)
1 tablespoon unsalted butter

240ml whole milk
1 medium onion
½ small bunch of parsley or chives, finely

chopped
360ml water

Preparation:

1. Preheat the air fryer at 40°C for 5 minutes. 2. Place smoked haddock in the milk and place the dish in the air fryer, cook for 5 minutes. Remove and set aside. 3. Take out Haddock from the milk and shred in pieces. Reserve the milk. 4. In a large pot, heat butter and sauté onions and potatoes. Add water and let it simmer on low for 15 minutes. 5. When potatoes are cooked, add the reserved milk and haddock pieces in the soup. 6. Dish out and serve warm.

Serving Suggestions: Serve with chopped parsley.

Variation Tip: You can add black pepper for added spiciness.

Nutritional Information per Serving:

Calories: 206 | Fat: 6g | Sat Fat: 4g | Carbohydrates: 21g | Fibre: 3g | Sugar: 6g | Protein: 17g

Delicious Beef Wellington Bites

Prep Time: 15 minutes | Cooking Time: 40 minutes | Servings: 6

Ingredients:

For the Beef:
455g (tenderloin)
1 tablespoon olive oil

½ teaspoon salt
¼ teaspoon black pepper

For the Mushroom Filling:
200g finely chopped button mushrooms
2 tablespoons olive oil
1 tablespoon regular soy sauce

½ onion, minced
1 pinch black pepper
70g pitted black olives

1 teaspoon dried oregano

For Beef Wellington Bites:
mustard, to taste

455g puff pastry

1 small egg, beaten (egg wash)

Preparation:

1. Cut beef into 2.5cm cubes. Toss beef cubes with salt, pepper and oil. 2. Preheat air fryer at 180°C for 10 minutes. Place beef cubes in the air fryer basket and cook for 5 minutes. Then flip the side and cook for another 5 minutes. Remove from the air fryer and set it aside covered with foil. 3. In a skillet, heat one tablespoon of oil. Sauté onions and mushrooms along with soya sauce, oregano and black pepper. Cook for 5 minutes and then remove from heat. Add olives and process the mixture in a food processor. 4. Unroll the puff pastry and cut in 12 small squares. Spread mustard and mushroom mixture from the back of the spoon. Put a beef cube in the middle of each square. Fold the puff pastry on each beef cube. 5. Place the beef wellington bites in the air fryer basket. Cook for 20 minutes. Brush egg wash after first 10 minutes. 6. Remove from the air fryer once they are golden brown.

Serving Suggestions: Serve with your favorite dipping sauce.

Variation Tip: You can also add other Italian seasoning for taste variation.

Nutritional Information per Serving:

Calories: 188 | Fat: 14g | Sat Fat: 3g | Carbohydrates: 10g | Fibre: 1g | Sugar: 1g | Protein: 7g

Mushroom and Prosciutto on Toast

Prep Time: 10 minutes | Cooking Time: 10 minutes | Servings: 4

Ingredients:

4 large slices of sourdough bread
4 slices prosciutto
Knob of butter

1 tbsp olive oil
100g sliced mushrooms
4 tablespoon crème fraiche

1 garlic clove, crushed
Handful parsley leaves, finely chopped

Preparation:

1. Preheat air fryer at 180°C for 4 minutes. Place toast in the air fryer basket and spray with oil. Toast for 4 minutes. 2. Heat butter in a frying pan and add mushrooms. Sauté for 30 seconds and then add crème fraiche. When mushrooms are coated with cream, add garlic and cook for 2 minutes. 3. Add mushrooms on each slice of the toast. Top with parsley and prosciutto. 4. Dish out and serve right away.

Serving Suggestions: Serve with your favorite dip and garnish with chopped parsley

Variation Tip: You can also serve with cream cheese.

Nutritional Information per Serving:

Calories: 280 | Fat: 16g | Sat Fat: 8g | Carbohydrates: 28g | Fibre: 3g | Sugar: 1g | Protein: 9g

Potted Prawns with Bread

Prep Time: 10 minutes | Cooking Time: 12 minutes | Servings: 4

Ingredients:

350g prawns (clean and deveined)
100g unsalted butter
2 pinches of cayenne pepper

1 ciabatta loaf
1 tablespoon olive oil
1 pinch of grated nutmeg

1 lemon, cut into wedges, to serve

Preparation:

1. In a saucepan, melt butter over low heat. Add cayenne pepper and grated nutmeg. Then add prawns and cook for a minute. 2. From a slotted spoon take out the prawns and put them aside in a bowl. Pour the melted butter on top of prawns to cover them. Season with salt and pepper. 3. Preheat air fryer for 10 minutes at 175°C. 4. Place the bread slices in the air fryer basket and drizzle olive oil. 5. Once golden brown, dish out and serve with potted prawns.

Serving Suggestions: Serve topped with lemon wedges.

Variation Tip: You can skip nutmeg for taste variation.

Nutritional Information per Serving:

Calories: 301 | Fat: 18g | Sat Fat: 9g | Carbohydrates: 21g | Fibre: 1g | Sugar: 1g | Protein: 14g

Pineapple Sticks with Yogurt Dip

Prep Time: 15 minutes | Cooking Time: 10 minutes | Servings: 4

Ingredients:

For Pineapple Sticks:
½ of pineapple, chopped into 2.5cm sticks   25g desiccated coconut

For Yogurt Dip:
1 tablespoon fresh mint leaves, minced   240g vanilla yogurt

Preparation:

1. In a shallow dish, place the coconut. 2. Roll the pineapple sticks in the coconut evenly. 3. Position the pineapple sticks carefully in the Baking Pan. 4. Set the temperature knob of Cuisinart Air Fryer Toaster Oven to 200°C and timer to 10 minutes. 5. Cook for about 10 minutes and dish out. 6. For yogurt dip: In a bowl, merge together mint and yogurt.

Serving Suggestions: Serve pineapple sticks with yogurt dip.

Variation Tip: You can also serve with BBQ sauce.

Nutritional Information per Serving:

Calories: 142 | Fat: 4.9g | Sat Fat: 4.2g | Carbohydrates: 20.7g | Fibre: 2.7g | Sugar: 15.9g | Protein: 4.6g

Air fry Brussels Sprouts with Bacon

Prep Time: 5 minutes | Cooking Time: 13 minutes | Servings: 4

Ingredients:

180g fresh Brussels sprouts,
1 tsp vegetable oil

4 strips of bacon,
¼ teaspoon of chilli flakes

Salt and pepper seasoning

Preparation:

1. Preheat air fryer to 80°C for 8 minutes. 2. In a mixing bowl, toss Brussel sprouts with olive oil and chili flakes. 3. Place Brussel sprouts in the air fryer basket and cook for 8 minutes. Toss them halfway through to the cook time. Once done, remove from the air fryer. 4. Next line bacon strips in the air fryer and cook at 80°C for 5 minutes or until they are crisp. 5. Toss the cooked Brussel sprouts with salt and pepper and top with crushed bacon. 6. Serve and Enjoy!

Serving Suggestions: Serve with yogurt dip.

Variation Tip: You can also add garlic powder for variation in flavor.

Nutritional Information per Serving:

Calories: 36 | Fat: 1g | Sat Fat: 0.2g | Carbohydrates: 2g | Fibre: 3g | Sugar: 2g | Protein: 2g

Crispy Fish and Chips

Prep Time: 5 minutes | Cooking Time: 18 minutes | Servings: 4

Ingredients:

455g cod fillet cut into strips
65g flour
½ teaspoon garlic powder
2 teaspoons paprika

½ teaspoon salt
¼ teaspoon black pepper
50g bread crumbs
1 large egg

Cooking oil spray
115g frozen chips

Preparation:

1. Preheat air fryer at 200°C for 10 minutes. 2. In a bowl add flour and season it with salt, pepper, garlic powder and paprika. 3. In another bowl beat the egg and set aside. 4. Take out bread crumbs in a relatively deep platter and set aside. 5. Pat dry fish fillets and coat them with flash then dunk them in the egg and lastly roll them in bread crumbs. 6. Spray oil on both sides of the fillets. 7. Place the fish fillets in the air fry basket in a single layer and cook them for 10 minutes, flipping them halfway through the cook time. 8. Next reduce the air fry temperature to 180°C and place the chips in the air fryer basket. Cook for 8 minutes and toss them halfway through the cook time. 9. Serve.

Serving Suggestions: Serve with tartar sauce and lemon wedges.

Variation Tip: You can also serve with marinara sauce for variation in flavor.

Nutritional Information per Serving:

Calories: 200 | Fat: 2g | Sat Fat: 1g | Carbohydrates: 18g | Fibre: 1g | Sugar: 1g | Protein: 24g

Cockle Pie

Prep Time: 10 minutes | Cooking Time: 15 minutes | Servings: 6

Ingredients:

2½ tablespoons butter
225g bacon
1 medium onion, chopped
40g plain flour

480ml milk
455g fresh cooked cockles
5 tablespoons dry white wine
3 tablespoons freshly chopped chives

50g fresh breadcrumbs
35g caerphilly cheese, grated

Preparation:

1. Preheat air fryer to 150°C. 2. In a saucepan, on medium heat, melt the butter and add onions and bacon. Saute for a minute. 3. Add flour and stir thoroughly. Turn the heat to low and add milk, stirring continuously till completely incorporated and thickened. 4. Next add cockles, wine and chives. Cook for another two minutes. 5. Transfer the mixture to one pie dish or individual ramekins or pie molds. 6. For topping: mix together cheese and breadcrumbs. 7. Put it on top of the cockle mixture, covering it completely. 8. Place the pie dish in the air fryer basket. If you are using individual pie dishes, then place them in a single layer and cook in batches. 9. Grill for 5 minutes, until golden brown from the top. 10. Serve immediately.

Serving Suggestions: Garnish with coriander or parsley.

Variation Tip: You can use any cheese as per your liking.

Nutritional Information per Serving:

Calories: 497 | Fat: 27.7g | Sat Fat: 11.6g | Carbohydrates: 29.9g | Fibre: 1.2g | Sugar: 5.2g | Protein: 29g

Grilled Leeks in Cheese Milk Sauce

Prep Time: 10 minutes | Cooking Time: 20 minutes | Servings: 6

Ingredients:

675g Leeks trimmed and cut into 3cm lengths
2 tablespoons butter

30g plain flour
240ml milk
Salt and freshly ground black pepper

Pinch nutmeg
50g Grated Cheddar Cheese

Preparation:

1. Preheat air fryer to 175°C for 10 minutes. 2. In a saucepan, steam Leeks for 5 minutes until cooked. Strain the water and place them in a pie dish which can fit into the air fryer. 3. For the cheese sauce, on a medium heat melt butter and sauté flour for one minute. Turn the heat to low and add milk, stirring continuously till completely incorporated and thickened. Add grated cheese and Season with salt, pepper and nutmeg. Stir until cheese is completely melted. 4. Pour the cheese sauce over the leeks and place the dish in the preheated air fryer for 10 minutes. 5. Serve hot and bubbling.

Serving Suggestions: Garnish with grated parmesan cheese.

Variation Tip: You can use Italian seasoning for the variation in taste.

Nutritional Information per Serving:

Calories: 181 | Fat: 8.2g | Sat Fat: 5g | Carbohydrates: 22.2g | Fibre: 2.2g | Sugar: 6.2g | Protein: 6g

Fish Cakes

Prep Time: 10 minutes | Cooking Time: 10 minutes | Servings: 6

Ingredients:

350g fish fillets
1 bay leaf
480ml milk
1 egg (beaten)

4 medium sized boiled potatoes
4 spring onions (sliced)
1 tbsp. dill (chopped)
35g breadcrumbs

Salt and pepper for seasoning
vegetable oil (for spraying)
1 tbsp. parsley (chopped)
Lime wedges (for garnishing)

Preparation:

1. Preheat air fryer to 200°C for 10 minutes. 2. In a pan heat milk with salt, pepper and bay leaf along with fish filets. Once milk is heated, turn the flame to low and poach for 5-10 minutes. 3. Remove the fish from the milk and leave it to cool. Reserve the milk. 4. Flake the fish and remove skin and bones. 5. Mash boiled potatoes by adding little amount of poaching milk. The consistency should not be soft. Add egg, parsley, fish, dill and parsley and mix with the wooden spoon. Season with freshly cracked black pepper and salt. 6. Make little disks and coat with bread crumbs. Spray the cakes with the oil on both sides. 7. Place the fish cakes in the pre heated air fryer for 10 minutes until golden brown. Flip them through the cooking time. 8. Serve warm and enjoy.

Serving Suggestions: Serve with lemon wedges and your favorite salad.

Variation Tip: You can spice it up by using cayenne pepper.

Nutritional Information per Serving:

Calories: 339 | Fat: 13.3g | Sat Fat: 3.7g | Carbohydrates: 41g | Fibre: 2.5g | Sugar: 5.1g | Protein: 16.7g

Halloumi Corn Bites

Prep Time: 10 minutes | Cooking Time: 10 minutes | Servings: 6

Ingredients:

100g grated haloumi cheese
375g corn kernels, drained, rinsed
2 eggs

40g self-rising flour
1 teaspoon lemon zest
2 tablespoons chopped fresh chives

Salt and pepper for seasoning
Olive oil for spraying

Preparation:

1. Preheat air fryer to 175°C for 10 minutes. 2. Dump haloumi, corn, eggs, chives, flour and lemon zest in a mixing bowl and mix well. Season with salt and pepper. 3. Spoon out the batter and place in the air fryer basket in a single layer. 4. Spray them with oil. 5. Cook in the preheated air fryer for 10 minutes until golden brown. Flip them through the cooking time. Repeat the same steps for the next batch. 6. Serve warm and enjoy.

Serving Suggestions: Serve with avocado yogurt dip and garnish with parsley.
Variation Tip: You can add chili flakes for some heat.
Nutritional Information per Serving:
Calories: 709 | Fat: 22.6g | Sat Fat: 9g | Carbohydrates: 117.1g | Fibre: 16.1g | Sugar: 19g | Protein: 34.3g

Golden Beef Pies

Prep Time: 30 minutes | Cooking Time: 1 Hour | Servings: 6

Ingredients:

455g beef mince
2 tablespoons vegetable oil
1 tablespoon tomato purée
1 onion, chopped

1½ tablespoons plain flour, plus extra for dusting
60g mushrooms, chopped
1 teaspoon Worcestershire sauce

270ml beef stock
350g of ready-made short crust pastry
For egg wash – 1 egg lightly beaten

Preparation:

1. In a pan heat oil and saute onions till they turn translucent. Then add flour and cook for a minute. 2. Add beef mince along with tomato puree and Worcestershire sauce. Then add chopped mushrooms and beef stock. Cover and cook for 30- 40 minutes till all the water evaporates and beef is cooked. 3. Preheat air fryer to 200°C for 10 minutes. 4. Unroll the pastry crust, roll out with the rolling pin and cut out 12 circles. Line 6 circles in a small muffin tray or individual pastry tins. 5. Spoon out the beef filling and cover the pies with the remaining 6 circles. Make a small slit on the cover. 6. Brush all the pies with the egg wash 7. Line the pies in the air fryer for 20 minutes until golden brown. Once done remove from the air fryer and cook the second batch. 8. Serve warm and enjoy.

Serving Suggestions: Serve with yogurt dip.
Variation Tip: You can top it up with grated cheese for taste variation.
Nutritional Information per Serving:
Calories: 625 | Fat: 36.6g | Sat Fat: 9.3g | Carbohydrates: 38.8g | Fibre: 2g | Sugar: 2.2g |

Chapter 3 Vegetable and Sides Recipes

Buttered Peas

Prep Time: 5 minutes | Cooking Time: 35 minutes | Servings: 6

Ingredients:

225g peas
25g salted butter, cubed

½ lemon, juiced
¼ small bunch of mint, finely chopped

Salt and pepper for seasoning

Preparation:

1. In saucepan cook peas with 600 ml of water until tender. Let it simmer for 30 minutes. Stir it occasionally. 2. Once the water reduces mash peas. Stir butter, mint and lemon. Remove from heat and season with salt and pepper. 3. Put them in a bowl and place in the air fryer for 5 minutes at 120°C. 4. Put a knob of butter on top and serve.

Serving Suggestions: You can serve it with chips.
Variation Tip: You can use dried peas. soak them overnight and then follow the same steps.
Nutritional Information per Serving:
Calories: 70 | Fat: 4g | Sat Fat: 2.5g | Carbohydrates: 6.6g | Fibre: 2.3g | Sugar: 2.5g | Protein: 2.4g

Cheese Cauliflower

Prep Time: 15 minutes | Cooking Time: 20 minutes | Servings: 4

Ingredients:

455g cauliflower florets
530ml milk

50g butter
100g grated cheddar

4 tablespoons flour
2-3 tablespoons breadcrumbs.

Preparation:

1. Preheat air fryer to 85°C. 2. In a large saucepan boil water and cook cauliflower for 2 minutes. Drain and transfer them in a heat proof dish. 3. In another saucepan heat butter and add flour in it. Mix well and turn the heat to low. Slowly add milk and cook until the sauce thickens. 4. Reserve some cheese and add the remaining in the sauce. Turn off the heat and mix the sauce until cheese melts. 5. Drizzle the sauce over cauliflower and top it with the grated cheese and breadcrumbs. 6. Place the dish in the air fryer and cook for 20 minutes. 7. Serve immediately

Serving Suggestions: Serve with green salad.
Variation Tip: Add in some cayenne pepper for taste enhancement.
Nutritional Information per Serving:
Calories: 289 | Fat: 16.7g | Sat Fat: 10.3g | Carbohydrates: 21.7g | Fibre: 3.2g | Sugar: 9.3g | Protein: 15g

Thyme Parsnip Soup

Prep Time: 30 minutes | Cooking Time: 10 minutes | Servings: 2

Ingredients:

250g 240 parsnips
1 tablespoon olive oil
1 tablespoon honey

Few sprigs fresh thyme
Salt and black pepper for seasoning
720ml vegetable stock

2 tablespoon cream (to garnish)

Preparation:

1. Preheat Air fryer at 145°C for 10 minutes. 2. Peel and cut parsnips in fingers. 3. Toss them with honey and oil along with the sprigs of thyme. Season it with salt and pepper. 4. Place them in a dish and cook in the air fryer for 10 minutes until crisp. Stir them halfway through the cook time. 5. Transfer the parsnips in the blender (Discarding the sprigs of thyme). Blend with vegetable stock until smooth. 6. If desired, serve topped with cream and fresh thyme leaves. 7. Dish out and serve warm.

Serving Suggestions: You can serve with crispy bread and garnish cayenne pepper.
Variation Tip: You can also add beef stock instead of vegetable stock.
Nutritional Information per Serving:
Calories: 240 | Fat: 8.6g | Sat Fat: 1.7g | Carbohydrates: 52g | Fibre: 10.1g | Sugar: 21.9g | Protein: 2.7g

Traditional Rumbled Thumps

Prep Time: 15 minutes | Cooking Time: 20 minutes | Servings: 6

Ingredients:

75g unsalted butter
525g leftover mashed potatoes
225g cabbage, finely sliced

350g mashed turnips
Salt, to taste
Pepper, to taste

25g grated cheddar cheese

Preparation:

1. Preheat air fryer at 180°C for 15 minutes. 2. Sauté sliced cabbage with butter on medium heat. Sauté till it is soft. 3. In a mixing bowl combine cabbage, mashed potatoes and turnips along with salt and pepper. 4. Transfer these in a small dish and top with grated cheese. 5. Cover with foil and cook in the air fryer for 15 minutes. Remove the foil and cook for another 5 minutes. 6. Serve piping hot as a side and enjoy.

Serving Suggestions: Garnish with chopped fresh thyme.

Variation Tip: You can also use breadcrumbs in the topping to make it crispier.

Nutritional Information per Serving:

Calories: 248 | Fat: 13g | Sat Fat: 8g | Carbohydrates: 29g | Fibre: 5g | Sugar: 4g | Protein: 5g

Cheese Leek Sausages

Prep Time: 30 minutes | Cooking Time: 20 min | Servings: 12

Ingredients:

2 large leeks, sliced
50g butter
350g breadcrumbs, divided
4 large eggs, separated

2 teaspoons thyme leaves
350g Caerphilly cheddar, finely grated
50g plain flour, for dusting
1 heaped tablespoon Dijon mustard

Salt and pepper, to taste
120ml vegetable oil for spraying

Preparation:

1. In a pan melt butter and fry leeks until they are soft. Set it aside and let it cool. 2. In a mixing bowl, combine 300g of breadcrumbs, egg yolks, cheese, thyme, mustard and leeks. Season the mixture with salt and pepper. 3. Shape the mixture in the form of sausages and place in a tray. Freeze them for 10 minutes. 4. Preheat air fryer for 20 minutes at 175°C. 5. Keep flour, remaining bread crumbs and whisked egg whites in separate shallow bowls. 6. Coat the sausages with flour, dunk in eggs and then roll in bread crumbs. 7. Line them in the pre heated air fryer basket and spray oil on them. 8. Cook for 20 minutes, flipping halfway through the cook time. 9. Dish out and serve warm.

Serving Suggestions: Serve with any chutney or ketchup.

Variation Tip: You can also add mozzarella cheese for cheesier flavor.

Nutritional Information per Serving:

Calories: 639 | Fat: 23.6g | Sat Fat: 16g | Carbohydrates: 64.4g | Fibre: 9.3g | Sugar: 19.3g | Protein: 31g

Tasty Scottish Stovies

Prep Time: 20 minutes | Cooking Time: 1 hour | Servings: 6

Ingredients:

30g Lard
1 onion, finely chopped
300g swede cubes

1 celery stick, finely chopped
455g leftover roast meat, cubed
675g potatoes, cut in cubes

500ml beef stock

Preparation:

1. In a dish combine lard, potatoes, celery and swede and beef stock. Cover with foil and cook in the air fryer for 20 minutes at 175°C. The lard should be completely melted and the vegetables should be soft. 2. Once done, dump all the vegetables in a saucepan, along with meat and the remaining beef stock. Bring it to boil on medium heat and then turn the heat low. 3. Let it simmer on low heat for another 40 minutes. 4. Dish out and serve.

Serving Suggestions: Serve with coriander leaves on top.

Variation Tip: You can use chicken or lamb meat instead of leftover beef.

Nutritional Information per Serving:

Calories: 418 | Fat: 23g | Sat Fat: 10g | Carbohydrates: 23g | Fibre: 4g | Sugar: 6g | Protein: 28g

Cheese and Leek tart

Prep Time: 10 minutes | Cooking Time: 20 minutes | Servings: 2

Ingredients:

2 large leeks, sliced
225g sheet ready-rolled puff pastry
1 tablespoon olive oil

2 strips bacon, chopped
2 slices firm Welsh goat's cheese
1 tablespoon crème fraîche

1 tablespoon mustard paste
Salt and pepper, to taste

Preparation:

1. Preheat air fryer at 200°C for 15 minutes. 2. Heat the oil in a frying pan, sauté leeks for a minute then add the bacon and cook for another 5 minutes. Season with salt and pepper. Set aside. 3. Unroll the pastry and cut out circles of the size of the tart tins. Put them in the tins and press the edges. 4. Mix the mustard and crème fraiche together, and spread in the lined pastry. Spoon leeks and bacon mixture then top it with goat's cheese. 5. Place these tarts in the air fryer and cook for 15 minutes until the pastry is crisp and golden. 6. Dish out and serve warm.

Serving Suggestions: Serve topped with coriander.

Variation Tip: You can also add cheddar cheese for the topping.

Nutritional Information per Serving:

Calories: 647 | Fat: 45g | Sat Fat: 18g | Carbohydrates: 45g | Fibre: 4g | Sugar: 0g | Protein: 18g

Cheese Fennel and Mushrooms Tartlets

Prep Time: 30 minutes | Cooking Time: 15 minutes | Servings: 4

Ingredients:

200g short crust pastry
For the Filling

150g mushrooms
1 bulb fennel, sliced and blanched
1 red onion, sliced
6 cloves garlic, lightly crushed

100ml whipping cream
Light olive oil
100g unsalted butter,
1 tablespoon chopped fresh chives

1 tablespoon lemon juice
1 tablespoon chopped parsley
Grated cheese
Salt and pepper, to taste

Preparation:

1. Grease tartlet tins of 10 cm diameter. 2. Roll out the pastry and cut out the circle of the size of the tins. Line the pastry in the tins and chill it in the fridge for 10 minutes. 3. Preheat the air fryer at 190°C with 10 minutes. Then place the tins in the air fryer for 10 minutes. Once golden brown, remove from the air fryer and set aside. 4. Set the temperature of the air fryer at 220°C. 5. Toss all the vegetables with salt, pepper, garlic and olive oil and place them in a dish. Air fry the vegetables for 5 minutes until lightly browned. 6. For the sauce: In a small pan bring cream to a boil and add the butter, herbs, salt and pepper, lemon juice along with 2 cloves of chopped garlic. 7. Fill the pre-baked tartlet shell with the vegetable mixture, top it with grated cheese and heat them in the air fryer at 220°C for 3 minutes. Remove from the air fryer and top with the sauce. 8. Serve and Enjoy!

Serving Suggestions: Garnish mushrooms and parsley.

Variation Tip: You can also serve it with herby salad.

Nutritional Information per Serving:

Calories: 648 | Fat: 53.5g | Sat Fat: 26.2g | Carbohydrates: 38.8g | Fibre: 3.6g | Sugar: 4.5g | Protein: 6g

Thyme Pumpkin Soup

Prep Time: 10 minutes | Cooking Time: 30 minutes | Servings: 6

Ingredients:

1 large white onion, chopped
1 medium pumpkin,
415ml coconut milk
1 piece of root ginger, finely chopped

2 garlic cloves, finely chopped
Salt and freshly ground black pepper
½ Scotch bonnet chilli, seeds removed, chopped

4–5 sprigs thyme
Breadfruit or sweet potato chunks, to taste (optional)
Oil for spraying

Preparation:

1. Cut pumpkin in 2.5cm cubes. 2. Toss pumpkin cubes with onion, chili, salt, black pepper, ginger and garlic along with thyme. Spray oil on the vegetables and mix well. 3. Place these vegetables in the air fryer and cook for 10 minutes at 175°C. 4. Once pumpkin cubes are soft, put them in the saucepan and pour 415 ml. water. Bring to a boil on medium heat and cook until pumpkin cubes are mushy. 5. Next add the coconut milk let the soup simmer 5–10 minutes. 6. Serve hot in bowls.

Serving Suggestions: Garnish with basil leaves, parsley and chili flakes.
Variation Tip: You can add bread fruit chunks or sweet potato for taste variation.
Nutritional Information per Serving:
Calories: 223 | Fat: 19.3g | Sat Fat: 15.2g | Carbohydrates: 13.8g | Fibre: 4.6g | Sugar: 6.1g | Protein: 2.9g

All-Vegetable Toad in The Hole

Prep Time: 10 minutes | Cooking Time: 15 minutes | Servings: 8

Ingredients:

1 tablespoon Dijon mustard
2 large eggs, lightly beaten
180ml whole milk
½ tablespoon unsalted butter
3 tablespoons olive oil, divided
2⅛ unbleached flour

30g whole-wheat flour
100g mushrooms
10 cherry tomatoes
1 small red onion, sliced.
150g chopped red pepper
150g sliced yellow pepper

85g sliced courgette
1 tablespoon chopped thyme
¾ teaspoon salt
½ teaspoon black pepper
3 garlic cloves, thinly sliced
15g thinly sliced basil

Preparation:

1. In a mixing bowl whisk eggs, milk, mustard, flour and wheat flour along with 1 tablespoons of oil. Once well combined keep it aside. 2. Preheat the air fryer at 200°C for 10 minutes 3. In a pan over medium heat, melt butter and sauté onions till lightly browned. Add the rest of the vegetables one by one except for the tomatoes and cook for 5 – 10 minutes. once the vegetables are soft, add tomatoes and stir. Season it with salt and pepper and remove from heat. Set aside. 4. In a heat proof dish pour the flour mixture and then place the vegetables in it. 5. Place the dish in the air fryer and cook for 15 minutes until it is set and lightly browned. 6. Remove from the air fryer. Serve warm and enjoy.

Serving Suggestions: you can drizzle some olive oil on top. Garnish with basil leaves.
Variation Tip: You can add cayenne pepper.
Nutritional Information per Serving:
Calories: 272 | Fat: 13g | Sat Fat: 4g | Carbohydrates: 2g | Fibre: 4g | Sugar: 8g | Protein: 9g

Pea and Mint Soup with Ham

Prep Time: 20 minutes | Cooking Time: 10 minutes | Servings: 4

Ingredients:

445ml water
drizzle olive oil
455g fresh peas

large handful fresh mint, leaves only
salt and freshly ground black pepper
210ml crème fraîche

4 slices ham

Preparation:

1. Boil water in a large pot and add the mint leaves and peas. Cook for 2-3 minutes. 2. Strain the mint and peas and reserve the liquid. 3. Blend peas and mint in a blender with oil until smooth. 4. Season with salt and pepper and drizzle some more oil. 5. Add crème fraîche to the blender for a few seconds, until combined. 6. Air fry Ham slices at 175°C or 4 minutes until crisp. Garnish on the soup. 7. Serve warm and enjoy.

Serving Suggestions: Serve with a dash of cream and some mint leaves on top.

Variation Tip: You can use croutons for serving.

Nutritional Information per Serving:

Calories: 186 | Fat: 6.4g | Sat Fat: 3g | Carbohydrates: 21.3g | Fibre: 7.7g | Sugar: 7.6g | Protein: 12g

Cheese Potato & Lentil Pie

Prep Time: 30 minutes | Cooking Time: 55 minutes | Servings: 6

Ingredients:

300g ready-made shortcrust pastry
120g dried red lentils
120g carrots, grated
240ml vegetable stock

85g frozen sweetcorn kernels
3 potatoes, thinly sliced
45g frozen peas
1 teaspoon Dijon mustard

½ teaspoon dried thyme
Salt and Black pepper
1 egg
135g cheddar cheese, grated

Preparation:

1. Lightly grease pie dish that first in the air fryer. Roll the crust and place it in the pie dish. 2. Preheat Air fryer at 150°C for 10 minutes and then cook the pie crust for 10 minutes until golden brown. 3. In a saucepan, add stock and lentils and cook for 15 minutes on medium heat. Once done drain the lentils. 4. Defrost frozen vegetables. 5. In a mixing bowl combine lentils along with all the vegetables, mustard, salt, pepper and thyme. 6. Mix egg and cheese in a bowl, reserve some cheese for the topping. 7. When the pastry is done, arrange potato slices in the base then fill it with the lentil mixture and top it with the cheese and egg topping. Garnish with reserved cheese and put it back in the air fryer for 30 minutes at 150°C until firm to touch. 8. Serve warm and enjoy.

Serving Suggestions: You can garnish with freshly ground black pepper.

Variation Tip: You can use oregano instead of thyme as well.

Nutritional Information per Serving:

Calories: 455 | Fat: 22.7g | Sat Fat: 4.7g | Carbohydrates: 46.9g | Fibre: 9.4g | Sugar: 2.2g | Protein: 15.8g

Herby Veggie Balls

Prep Time: 10 minutes | Cooking Time: 15 minutes | Servings: 8

Ingredients:

125g self-rising flour
½ tablespoon oregano

½ tablespoon chives
150g vegetable suet

½ teaspoon salt
180ml water

Preparation:

1. Preheat the air fryer at 150°C. 2. In a bowl combine all the ingredients and mix well to form a dough. 3. Make 8 small balls out of the dough. 4. Place the balls in a dish and place in the air fryer. Cook for 10 minutes. Flip the balls and cook for another 5 minutes. 5. Serve warm and enjoy.

Serving Suggestions: Serve with any meat curry and fresh salad.

Variation Tip: Vegetable Suet can be replaced by vegetable shortening.

Nutritional Information per Serving:

Calories: 191 | Fat: 12g | Sat Fat: 3g | Carbohydrates: 18g | Fibre: 1g | Sugar: 1g | Protein: 3g

Vegetarian Cheese Bean Patties

Prep Time: 20 minutes | Cooking Time: 30 minutes | Servings: 6

Ingredients:

175g marinated artichoke hearts (drained)
65g parmesan cheese, grated
225g cannellini beans, drained
1 egg

2 small slices bread
Salt and Black pepper
Few sprigs fresh parsley
1 teaspoon lemon juice

Spray oil
6 tablespoons dried breadcrumbs

Preparation:

1. In a food processor add beans along with grated parmesan, bread, salt, pepper and parsley. Pulse to form a coarse mixture 2. Next add artichokes, egg, lemon juice and some breadcrumbs. Pulse again. The mixture should be able to hold the shape. 3. Preheat the air fryer at 200°C for 30 minutes. 4. Spray oil in a dish that will fit in the air fryer. 5. Keep bread crumbs in a separate bowl. Make small patties of the mixture and roll it with the bread crumbs. 6. Put the patties in the dish and spray with oil again. 7. Place the dish in the air fryer and cook for about 30 minutes, flipping them half way through to the cook time. 8. Serve warm and enjoy.
Serving Suggestions: Serve with Lime wedges.
Variation Tip: You can add grated carrots as well.
Nutritional Information per Serving:

Calories: 159 | Fat: 7.1g | Sat Fat: 2.1g | Carbohydrates: 16.9g | Fibre: 4.2g | Sugar: 2.1g | Protein: 8.1g

Roasted Potatoes

Prep Time: 10 minutes | Cooking Time: 15 minutes | Servings: 8

Ingredients:

1.1kg potatoes, cut in cubes
1 tsp. salt

1 tsp. pepper
50ml oil

Preparation:

1. Parboil potatoes in a large pan. 2. Drain and spread them on a tea towel. 3. Preheat air fryer for 15 minutes at 200°C. 4. Toss the potatoes with oil, salt and pepper. 5. Place them in the air fryer in a single layer and cook for about 15 minutes. Shake them halfway through. 6. Once crisp and golden brown, remove from the air fryer. 7. Serve warm and enjoy.
Serving Suggestions: Serve with Italian seasoning.
Variation Tip: You can garnish Italian basil seasoning for variation in taste.
Nutritional Information per Serving:

Calories: 258 | Fat: 11.6g | Sat Fat: 1.5g | Carbohydrates: 35.9g | Fibre: 5.6g | Sugar: 2.6g | Protein: 3.9g

Vegan Shepherd's Pie

Prep Time: 10 minutes | Cooking Time: 50 minutes | Servings: 4

Ingredients:

1 tablespoon olive oil
1 large onion, halved and sliced
455g carrot cubes
2 tablespoon thyme chopped

210ml red wine
300g can chopped tomatoes
2 vegetable stock cubes
300g can of green lentils

900g boiled sweet potatoes
25g butter
75g cheddar, grated

Preparation:

1. In a pan heat oil and sauté onions until golden brown. 2. Add carrots and thyme along with red wine and tomatoes. Stir and add 120 ml of water and vegetable stock cubes. Let it simmer for 10 minutes. 3. Next add lentils and cook for 10 minutes until they become mushy. Dish out in a pie dish that fits in the air fryer. 4. Mash sweet potatoes with butter and mix until smooth. Spread mashed potatoes on top of the vegetables and cover with cheddar cheese. 5. Preheat air fryer to 150°C for 20 minutes. Place the pie dish in the air fryer and cook for 20 minutes until golden brown.
Serving Suggestions: Garnish with coriander and serve with crusted bread.
Variation Tip: You can also use any other vegetables of your choice.
Nutritional Information per Serving:

Calories: 540 | Fat: 16g | Sat Fat: 8g | Carbohydrates: 66g | Fibre: 16g | Sugar: 33g | Protein: 16g

Chapter 4 Fish and Seafood Recipes

Bacon-Wrapped Oyster

Prep Time: 10 minutes | Cooking Time: 13 minutes | Servings: 8

Ingredients:

16 slices bacon, thin-cut

32 small oysters, shucked

Lime or lemon wedges, for serving

Preparation:

1. Switch the temperature of the Air fryer to 175°C. 2. Air fry the bacon for 5 minutes, until they are cooked but not crispy. 3. Wrap half piece of bacon around the oyster and fasten with a toothpick. 4. Cook in the Air fryer for about 8 minutes, turning once in between. 5. Trickle with lemon or lime juice and serve warm.

Serving Suggestions: You can serve topped with lime or lemon wedges.

Variation Tip: You can use scallops instead of oyster too.

Nutritional Information per Serving:

Calories: 551 | Fat: 25g | Sat Fat: 8g | Carbohydrates: 24g | Fibre: 1g | Sugar: 1g | Protein: 54g

Crispy Haddock and French Fries

Prep Time: 15 minutes | Cooking Time: 20 minutes | Servings: 4

Ingredients:

455g haddock fillets, fresh and cut into smaller pieces
455g French fries, frozen
1 egg, large

2 teaspoons paprika
110g panko bread crumbs
¼ teaspoon black pepper
65g flour

½ teaspoon garlic powder
½ teaspoon salt

Preparation:

1. Switch the temperature of the Air fryer to 200°C. 2. Air fry frozen French fries for 10 minutes, turning once in between. 3. Now, put the bread crumbs in a bowl, and whisk egg in another bowl. 4. In the third bowl, merge flour with paprika, garlic powder, salt and pepper and stir well. 5. Dredge the haddock into the flour mixture, and then dip into the egg mixture. 6. Finally, coat evenly with the breadcrumbs and spray lightly with oil. 7. Layer the haddock in the air fryer basket and cook for 10 minutes, flipping halfway. 8. Dish out the haddock and serve with the French fries.

Serving Suggestions: Serve with lemon and tartar sauce.

Variation Tip: You can also use cod instead of haddock.

Nutritional Information per Serving:

Calories: 684 | Fat: 26g | Sat Fat: 8g | Carbohydrates: 77g | Fibre: 8g | Sugar: 8g | Protein: 36g

Potted Butter Scallops

Prep Time: 10 minutes | Cooking Time: 8 minutes | Servings: 6

Ingredients:

2 pinches of cayenne pepper
115g butter, unsalted

½ teaspoon nutmeg, grated
340g scallops

Preparation:

1. Switch the temperature of the Air fryer to 200°C. 2. Merge the scallops with butter, cayenne pepper, and nutmeg in a bowl. 3. Move the scallops to Air fryer and air fry for about 8 minutes. 4. Shift the scallops into the ramekins and refrigerate overnight to set. 5. Serve the next day with toasted slices.

Serving Suggestions: Serve topped with lemon wedges.

Variation Tip: You can also use prawns instead of scallops.

Nutritional Information per Serving:

Calories: 263 | Fat: 19.1g | Sat Fat: 13.7g | Carbohydrates: 8.2g | Fibre: 0.4g |
Sugar: 0.4g | Protein: 14.4g

Finnan Haddie

Prep Time: 5 minutes | Cooking Time: 35 minutes | Servings: 6

Ingredients:

2 tablespoons flour
900g haddock fillets, smoked

55g butter, melted
480ml warm milk

Preparation:

1. Switch the temperature of the Air fryer to 160°C. 2. Merge smoked haddock with flour, melted butter, and milk in a bowl. 3. Move this mixture into the baking pan and put it into the Air fryer. 4. Air fry for about 35 minutes and dish out to serve.

Serving Suggestions: Serve garnished with parsley.

Variation Tip: You can also add in some oregano for taste variation.

Nutritional Information per Serving:

Calories: 294 | Fat: 11g | Sat Fat: 6g | Carbohydrates: 6g | Fibre: 0g | Sugar: 4g | Protein: 41g

Virgin Islands Fish and Fungi

Prep Time: 5 minutes | Cooking Time: 40 minutes | Servings: 6

Ingredients:

Virgin Islands Style Fish
2 medium onions, chopped
2kg fish, scaled and gutted
1 tomato, chopped

3 tablespoons lime juice
2 teaspoons butter
1 tablespoon vinegar

480ml water

Okra Fungi
600ml boiling water
1 (250g) package frozen okra

240g yellow polenta, ground fine
¼ teaspoon salt

2 tablespoons butter
Black pepper, to taste

Preparation:

1. Switch the temperature of the Air fryer to 160°C. 2. Merge fish with butter and move into the Air fryer. 3. Air fry for about 10 minutes, flipping once in between. 4. Transfer the fish into a saucepan along with remaining ingredients for fish and cook for about 20 minutes. 5. Boil the frozen okra until barely tender. 6. In another saucepan, boil water. 7. Merge about 40 g of the polenta with 180 ml water in another bowl. 8. Put this mixture back into the boiling water and cook for 1 minute, stirring constantly. 9. Add okra to polenta and stir well. 10. Then, add in the butter, salt and black pepper. 11. Simmer for about 5 minutes more and dish out to serve.

Serving Suggestions: Serve with mashed potatoes.

Variation Tip: You can use any kind of white fish.

Nutritional Information per Serving:

Calories: 621 | Fat: 24.8g | Sat Fat: 4.8g | Carbohydrates: 31.4g | Fibre: 4.7g | Sugar: 2.9g | Protein: 69.9g

Halibut with Yuca Fries

Prep Time: 5 minutes | Cooking Time: 20 minutes | Servings: 8

Ingredients:

455g yuca, peeled and cut into sticks
2 teaspoons paprika
65g flour
½ teaspoon garlic powder

¼ teaspoon black pepper
55g panko bread crumbs
Cooking oil spray
½ teaspoon salt

1 large egg beaten
455g halibut fillets, cut into strips

Preparation:

1. Switch the temperature of the Air fryer to 200°C. 2. In a small bowl, merge flour with garlic powder, paprika, salt, and black pepper. 3. Now, put the bread crumbs in a bowl, and whisk egg in another bowl. 4. Dredge the fish into the flour mixture, and then dip into the egg mixture. 5. Finally, coat evenly with the breadcrumbs and spray lightly with oil. 6. Layer the fish in the air fryer basket and cook for 12 minutes, flipping halfway. 7. Dish out the fish and add yuca fries to the Air fryer basket. 8. Air fry for about 8 minutes and dish out to serve with the fish.

Serving Suggestions: You can serve with tartar sauce.

Variation Tip: You can use haddock or cod instead of halibut.

Nutritional Information per Serving:

Calories: 200 | Fat: 18g | Sat Fat: 1g | Carbohydrates: 18g | Fibre: 1g | Sugar: 1g | Protein: 24g

Buttered Kippers

Prep Time: 5 minutes | Cooking Time: 10 minutes | Servings: 4

Ingredients:

115g butter

4 kippers

1 bunch of curly parsley, chopped

Granary bread

1 lemon, cut into wedges

Preparation:

1. Switch the temperature of the Air fryer to 200°C. 2. In a saucepan, put the butter and cook until it is nutty brown. 3. Position the kippers in a baking tray and top with browned butter. 4. Move the baking tray inside the Air Fryer and air fry for 10 minutes, flipping once in between. 5. Dish out and serve with butter, parsley, and granary toast slices.

Serving Suggestions: Serve topped with lemon wedges.

Variation Tip: You can also add celery instead of parsley.

Nutritional Information per Serving:

Calories: 322 | Fat: 11.8g | Sat Fat: 2.2g | Carbohydrates: 14.6g | Fibre: 4.4g | Sugar: 8g | Protein: 17.3g

Breaded Fish with Tartar Sauce

Prep Time: 12 minutes | Cooking Time: 12 minutes | Servings: 3

Ingredients:

1 medium lemon, quartered

455g breaded fish fillets, frozen

For tartar sauce:

3 tablespoons dill pickles, chopped

6 tablespoons mayonnaise

Preparation:

1. Switch the temperature of the Air fryer to 175°C. 2. Layer the fish fillets in Air fryer and air fry for 12 minutes, flipping once in between. 3. Meanwhile, merge dill pickles and mayonnaise to make tartar sauce. 4. Dish out the fish fillets and serve squeezed with lemon.

Serving Suggestions: Serve with tartar sauce.

Variation Tip: You can also make the breading from scratch.

Nutritional Information per Serving:

Calories: 280 | Fat: 10g | Sat Fat: 1g | Carbohydrates: 31g | Fibre: 1g | Sugar: 2g | Protein: 17g

Beer Battered Cod

Prep Time: 10 minutes | Cooking Time: 12 minutes | Servings: 4

Ingredients:

2 tablespoons cornflour

125g flour

½ teaspoon baking soda

1 egg, beaten

½ teaspoon paprika

¼ teaspoon black pepper, freshly ground

4 pieces cod, 4.5 cm thick

150ml beer

90g flour

1 teaspoon salt

1 pinch cayenne pepper

vegetable oil spray

Preparation:

1. Switch the temperature of the Air fryer to 200°C. 2. In a large bowl, merge 125g of flour, cornflour, and baking soda. 3. Stir in the beer and egg and thoroughly mix. 4. Wrap the bowl and refrigerate for half an hour. 5. In a shallow pan, merge 90g of flour, paprika, salt, black pepper and cayenne pepper. 6. Coat the fish with batter and then dredge in the seasoned flour. 7. Position the fish fillets in the Air fryer basket and spray with vegetable oil. 8. Air fry for about 12 minutes and dish out to serve.

Serving Suggestions: Serve with French fries and coleslaw.

Variation Tip: You can also use salmon instead of cod.

Nutritional Information per Serving:

Calories: 442 | Fat: 3.5g | Sat Fat: 0.8g | Carbohydrates: 47.2g | Fibre: 1.7g | Sugar: 0.3g | Protein: 48.6g

Easy Crab Cakes

Prep Time: 5 minutes | Cooking Time: 10 minutes | Servings: 4

Ingredients:

250g crabs, finely chopped
Cooking spray
75g whole-wheat panko breadcrumbs
2 tablespoons Thai sweet chili sauce

1 large egg
¼ teaspoon ground pepper
3 tablespoons fresh coriander, finely chopped

2 tablespoons mayonnaise
⅛ teaspoon salt
2 lime wedges

Preparation:

1. Switch the temperature of the Air fryer to 200°C. 2. In a bowl, merge crab meat, panko, coriander, chili sauce, mayonnaise, egg, salt, and black pepper. 3. Mix well and form cakes 8cm in diameter. 4. Position the cakes inside the Air fryer basket and spray with cooking spray. 5. Air fry for about 10 minutes, flipping once in between. 6. Dish out and serve garnished with lemon wedges.
Serving Suggestions: Serve with tomato ketchup.
Variation Tip: You can use fish instead of crabs.
Nutritional Information per Serving:
Calories: 399 | Fat: 15.5g | Sat Fat: 2.1g | Carbohydrates: 27.9g | Fibre: 2.8g | Sugar: 9.8g | Protein: 34.6g

Spicy Lemon Fish

Prep Time: 5 minutes | Cooking Time: 30 minutes | Servings: 4

Ingredients:

1 lemon
2 Basa fish fillets, each cut into 4 pieces
Juice of 1 lemon
Salt, to taste

2 teaspoons oil, for brushing
4 teaspoons corn flour slurry
3 lettuce leaves
125g plain flour + for coating

2 teaspoons green chili sauce
1 egg white
1 teaspoon red chili sauce

Preparation:

1. Switch the temperature of the Air fryer to 180°C. 2. Put lemon slices in a bowl. 3. In another bowl, merge 125 g flour, salt, green chili sauce, 2 teaspoons oil, egg white, and 3 tablespoons water. Whisk well to form a smooth batter. 4. Spread flour in another plate. 5. Coat the fish fillets with the batter and dredge in the flour. 6. Grease olive oil on the Air fryer basket and layer the fish fillets in it. 7. Air fry for about 25 minutes, flipping twice in between. 8. Pour remaining batter in the pan with salt and corn flour slurry. 9. Add red chili sauce, lemon juice and slices. Cook until the sauce thickens. 10. In a serving platter, arrange lettuce leaves and top with fish and lemon sauce to serve.
Serving Suggestions: You can serve with tartar sauce or ketchup.
Variation Tip: You can also use butter instead of oil.
Nutritional Information per Serving:
Calories: 282 | Fat: 8.5g | Sat Fat: 3.6g | Carbohydrates: 38.3g | Fibre: 1.7g | Sugar: 2.2g | Protein: 13.2g

Simple Fish Fillets

Prep Time: 5 minutes | Cooking Time: 10 minutes | Servings: 4

Ingredients:

4 frozen fish fillets

Cooking oil spray

Preparation:

1. Switch the temperature of the Air fryer to 200°C. 2. Grease the Air fryer basket with cooking oil spray and layer with frozen fish fillets. 3. Air fry for about 10 minutes and dish out to serve.
Serving Suggestions: Serve garnished with chopped sage.
Variation Tip: You can use any brand of frozen fish.
Nutritional Information per Serving:
Calories: 156 | Fat: 13g | Sat Fat: 2g | Carbohydrates: 2g | Fibre: 0.3g | Sugar: 0.8g | Protein: 19g

Crispy Air Fryer Cod

Prep Time: 10 minutes | Cooking Time: 11 minutes | Servings: 2

Ingredients:

455g of cod
65g flour
2 teaspoons taco seasoning

¼ teaspoon cayenne pepper
⅛ teaspoon black pepper
1 egg

165g panko breadcrumbs
2 teaspoons old bay seasoning
½ teaspoon salt

Preparation:

1. Switch the temperature of the Air fryer to 200°C. 2. Put the flour in a bowl, and whisk egg in another bowl. 3. In the third bowl, merge panko breadcrumbs with salt, pepper, cayenne pepper, old bay seasoning, and taco seasoning and stir well. 4. Dredge the cod into the flour mixture, and then dip into the egg mixture. 5. Finally, coat evenly with the breadcrumbs mixture and spray lightly with oil. 6. Layer the cod in the air fryer basket and cook for 11 minutes, flipping halfway. 7. Dish out the cod and serve well.

Serving Suggestions: Serve inside the tacos.
Variation Tip: You can also add sour cream and cheese inside tacos.
Nutritional Information per Serving:
Calories: 598 | Fat: 6g | Sat Fat: 1.1g | Carbohydrates: 69.9g | Fibre: 6.9g | Sugar: 1.9g | Protein: 63.8g

Lemony Whole Seabass with Herb

Prep Time: 10 minutes | Cooking Time: 20 minutes | Servings: 4

Ingredients:

1 lemon, sliced
1 big seabass

35g fresh herbs, thyme and chives
1 teaspoon olive oil

Salt, to taste

Preparation:

1. Switch the temperature of the Air fryer to 200°C. 2. Carve slashes on both sides of the fish and rub the fish with olive oil and salt. 3. Stuff the lemon slices and herbs in the slashes. 4. Move the seabass in the Air fryer basket and air fry for about 20 minutes. 5. Dish out and serve hot.

Serving Suggestions: Serve with balsamic onions.
Variation Tip: You can use any fresh herbs of your choice.
Nutritional Information per Serving:
Calories: 138 | Fat: 4.5g | Sat Fat: 1g | Carbohydrates: 8g | Fibre: 3.8g | Sugar: 0.5g | Protein: 1.4g

Fried lemon Salmon

Prep Time: 5 minutes | Cooking Time: 12 minutes | Servings: 2

Ingredients:

2 tablespoons butter, unsalted
455g salmon fillets

1 lemon
1 teaspoon garlic parsley salt

Preparation:

1. Switch the temperature of the Air fryer to 200°C. 2. Dust garlic parsley salt on the salmon fillets and layer in the Air fryer basket. 3. Top with lemon slices and butter and air fry for about 12 minutes. 4. Dish out and serve warm.

Serving Suggestions: Serve with basil on top.
Variation Tip: Add red chili flakes to spice up the taste.
Nutritional Information per Serving:
Calories: 234 | Fat: 26g | Sat Fat: 9g | Carbohydrates: 5g | Fibre: 1g | Sugar: 1g | Protein: 45g

Roasted Salmon with Garlic Honey Sauce

Prep Time: 5 minutes | Cooking Time: 12 minutes | Servings: 4

Ingredients:

1 tablespoon oil
900g fresh salmon, cut into 4-5 fillets
2½ tablespoons soy sauce
1½ teaspoons rice vinegar

¼ teaspoon sesame oil
1½ teaspoons cornflour
¼ teaspoon lemon pepper
20g honey

3 cloves garlic, minced
1½ teaspoons cold water
1 teaspoon parsley

Preparation:

1. Switch the temperature of the Air fryer to 200°C. 2. Rub oil on the salmon fillets and layer them in the Air fryer basket. 3. Air fry for about 8 minutes and dish out. 4. In a bowl, merge honey, soy sauce, rice vinegar, garlic, sesame oil, cornflour, and water. 5. Transfer this mixture in a saucepan and cook until thickened over medium heat. 6. Brush salmon with this sauce and serve sprinkled with lemon pepper and parsley.

Serving Suggestions: Serve with ketchup.
Variation Tip: You can also serve it with cream cheese.
Nutritional Information per Serving:
Calories: 433 | Fat: 17.7g | Sat Fat: 2.5g | Carbohydrates: 25.8g | Fibre: 0.2g | Sugar: 23.4g | Protein: 44.9g

Smoked Haddock with Basmati Rice

Prep Time: 5 minutes | Cooking Time: 35 minutes | Servings: 8

Ingredients:

1 medium onion, finely chopped
55g butter
3 cardamom pods, split open
1 small cinnamon stick

400g basmati rice
185g smoked haddock fillet, un-dyed
3 tablespoons fresh parsley, chopped
¼ teaspoon turmeric

2 fresh bay leaves
960ml fish stock, ideally fresh
3 eggs, hard-boiled
1 lemon, cut into wedges, to garnish

Preparation:

1. Switch the temperature of the Air fryer to 200°C. 2. Grease the Air fryer basket with the cooking spray and haddock fillets. 3. Air fry for about 12 minutes and dish out in a plate. 4. In a saucepan, put butter and onions, and cook for about 5 minutes on medium heat. 5. Add cardamom pods, turmeric, cinnamon stick and bay leaves, then cook for 1 minute. 6. Add basmati rice and stir thoroughly. 7. Stir in the stock and salt and thoroughly boil. 8. Fasten the lid, switch the heat to low and cook for 12 minutes. 9. Flake the fish and get rid of the skin and bones. 10. Eliminate the bay leaves, cinnamon stick and cardamom pods from the rice. 11. Add chopped fish and eggs and cover again to cook for another 3 minutes. 12. Dust with a little salt and black pepper, and serve garnished with parsley and lemon wedges.

Serving Suggestions: Serve with mashed potatoes.
Variation Tip: You can also use chicken stock instead of fish stock.
Nutritional Information per Serving:
Calories: 284 | Fat: 8.8g | Sat Fat: 4.5g | Carbohydrates: 40.1g | Fibre: 1.6g | Sugar: 1g | Protein: 10.6g

Crispy Potato-Crusted Fish

Prep Time: 5 minutes | Cooking Time: 10 minutes | Servings: 3

Ingredients:

½ teaspoon paprika
40g flour

1 egg, beaten
25g salt and vinegar potato chips

60g mayonnaise
150g cod fillets

Preparation:

1. Switch the temperature of the Air fryer to 190°C. 2. Crush the salt and vinegar potato chips coarsely. 3. Put the flour and paprika in a bowl, and whisk egg and mayonnaise in another bowl. 4. In the third bowl, add crushed potato chips. 5. Dredge the fish into the flour mixture, and then dip into the egg mixture. 6. Finally, coat evenly with the potato chip mixture and spray lightly with oil. 7. Layer the fish in the air fryer basket and cook for 10 minutes, flipping halfway. 8. Dish out the fish and serve well.

Serving Suggestions: Serve with tartar sauce and lemon wedges.
Variation Tip: You can use haddock in this recipe.
Nutritional Information per Serving:
Calories: 210 | Fat: 9.2g | Sat Fat: 1.4g | Carbohydrates: 19.2g | Fibre: 0.9g | Sugar: 1.8g | Protein: 12.9g

Golden Cajun Fish Fillets

Prep Time: 5 minutes | Cooking Time: 14 minutes | Servings: 2

Ingredients:

2 teaspoons Cajun seasoning
2 tablespoons polenta

½ teaspoon paprika
Sea salt flakes, to taste

½ teaspoon garlic powder
2 white fish fillets

Preparation:

1. Switch the temperature of the Air fryer to 200°C. 2. Put all the ingredients in a Ziploc bag, seal it and shake well. 3. Position the fish in the Air fryer basket and air fry for about 14 minutes, flipping once in between. 4. Dish out and serve hot.
Serving Suggestions: Serve with peri peri sauce.
Variation Tip: You can use your favorite spices, herbs, and seasonings.
Nutritional Information per Serving:
Calories: 296 | Fat: 11.9g | Sat Fat: 1.8g | Carbohydrates: 6.7g | Fibre: 0.8g | Sugar: 0.3g | Protein: 38.5g

Air Fryer Lemony Halibut

Prep Time: 5 minutes | Cooking Time: 10 minutes | Servings: 4

Ingredients:

4 Halibut fillets
½ teaspoon black pepper

Salt, to taste
1 tablespoon lemon juice

1 tablespoon olive oil

Preparation:

1. Switch the temperature of the Air fryer to 180°C. 2. Squeeze the Halibut fillets with lemon juice, then dust with salt and pepper. 3. Brush one side of the Halibut fillets with olive oil and layer in the Air fryer basket. 4. Air fry for about 10 minutes and dish out to serve.
Serving Suggestions: Serve with garlic butter sauce.
Variation Tip: You can also use haddock or cod in this recipe.
Nutritional Information per Serving:
Calories: 100 | Fat: 2g | Sat Fat: 1g | Carbohydrates: 1g | Fibre: 1g | Sugar: 1g | Protein: 20g

Air Fryer Garlic Prawns

Prep Time: 5 minutes | Cooking Time: 12 minutes | Servings: 10

Ingredients:

1 large fresh garlic clove, minced
455g prawns, frozen, thawed or fresh
2 tablespoons butter, unsalted, cut into

small cubes
½ lemon, juiced
Salt and black pepper, to taste

1 tablespoon parsley, chopped to garnish

Preparation:

1. Switch the temperature of the Air fryer to 200°C. 2. Dust the prawns with salt and black pepper, add the garlic, spray with cooking oil and stir thoroughly. 3. Add butter to the prawns then layer them in the Air fryer tray. 4. Air fry for about 10 minutes, flipping once in between. 5. Dish out the prawns, squeeze with lemon juice and serve garnished with parsley.
Serving Suggestions: You can serve with Thai sweet chili sauce.
Variation Tip: You can serve with tartar sauce too.
Nutritional Information per Serving:
Calories: 169 | Fat: 8g | Sat Fat: 4g | Carbohydrates: 1g | Fibre: 1g | Sugar: 1g | Protein: 23g

Chapter 5 Chicken and Poultry Recipes

Italian Seasoned Chicken

Prep Time: 5 minutes | Cooking Time: 25 minutes | Servings: 4

Ingredients:

1 tablespoon Italian seasoning
1 teaspoon garlic powder

4 chicken breasts, boneless and skinless
1½ teaspoons salt

1 teaspoon paprika
1 tablespoon olive oil

Preparation:

1. Switch the temperature of the Air fryer to 200°C. 2. In a bowl, merge Italian seasoning, salt, garlic powder, and paprika. 3. Brush olive oil on chicken and dredge in the seasoning mixture. 4. Layer the chicken in the Air fryer basket and air fry for about 25 minutes, flipping once in between. 5. Dish out and serve warm.

Serving Suggestions: Serve topped with lemon wedges.
Variation Tip: You can also use butter instead of olive oil.
Nutritional Information per Serving:
Calories: 322 | Fat: 15.4g | Sat Fat: 3.7g | Carbohydrates: 1.2g | Fibre: 0.3g | Sugar: 0.5g | Protein: 42.5g

Easy Fried Chicken Legs

Prep Time: 35 minutes | Cooking Time: 20 minutes | Servings: 3

Ingredients:

½ teaspoon paprika
455g chicken legs
½ teaspoon parsley

¼ teaspoon onion powder
⅛ teaspoon garlic granules
Salt, to taste

¼ teaspoon black pepper

Preparation:

1. Switch the temperature of the Air fryer to 180°C. 2. In a bowl, merge chicken leg quarters with paprika, parsley, black pepper, onion powder, garlic granules and salt. Marinate for about 30 minutes. 3. Layer the chicken leg quarters in the Air fryer basket and air fry for about 20 minutes, flipping once in between. 4. Dish out and serve warm.

Serving Suggestions: Serve with potatoes and carrots.
Variation Tip: You can also make chicken breasts with this recipe.
Nutritional Information per Serving:
Calories: 359 | Fat: 27g | Sat Fat: 7g | Carbohydrates: 1g | Fibre: 1g | Sugar: 1g | Protein: 27g

Breaded Chicken Breast

Prep Time: 6 minutes | Cooking Time: 15 minutes | Servings: 2

Ingredients:

100g fresh breadcrumbs
2 large chicken breasts, skinless and boneless

¼ teaspoon salt
¼ teaspoon garlic powder
¾ teaspoon paprika

¼ teaspoon white pepper
¼ teaspoon onion powder
2 tablespoons olive oil

Preparation:

1. Switch the temperature of the Air fryer to 200°C. 2. Dust the chicken breasts with salt. 3. In a dish, merge breadcrumbs, pepper, garlic, onion and paprika. 4. Rub oil over chicken breasts and dredge in the breadcrumbs. 5. Layer the chicken breasts in the Air fryer basket and air fry for 15 minutes, flipping once in between. 6. Dish out and serve warm.

Serving Suggestions: Serve with pickled vegetables.
Variation Tip: You can use pork rinds instead of breadcrumbs.
Nutritional Information per Serving:
Calories: 302 | Fat: 6g | Sat Fat: 2g | Carbohydrates: 19g | Fibre: 2g | Sugar: 2g | Protein: 41g

Air Fryer BBQ Chicken Thighs

Prep Time: 10 minutes | Cooking Time: 30 minutes | Servings: 4

Ingredients:

8 small chicken thighs, skin on
1 tablespoon plain flour

1 tablespoon sunflower oil
1 teaspoon smoky BBQ

Preparation:

1. Switch the temperature of the Air fryer to 200°C. 2. In a bowl, merge flour with the seasoning. 3. Rub oil over chicken thighs and dredge in the seasoning. 4. Layer the chicken thighs in the Air fryer basket and air fry for about 30 minutes, flipping once in between. 5. Dish out and serve warm.

Serving Suggestions: Serve with steamed rice.

Variation Tip: You can also use chicken breasts instead of chicken thighs.

Nutritional Information per Serving:

Calories: 250 | Fat: 16g | Sat Fat: 4g | Carbohydrates: 4g | Fibre: 0.6g | Sugar: 0g | Protein: 22g

Air Fryer Turkey with Brandy Sauce

Prep Time: 5 minutes | Cooking Time: 50 minutes | Servings: 4

Ingredients:

For the Turkey
1.35kg turkey breast, bone-in
1 teaspoon salt
1 teaspoon sweet paprika

½ teaspoon black pepper
1 teaspoon dried thyme
1 teaspoon mixed Italian herbs

1 teaspoon garlic powder

For the Gravy
1 tablespoon flour
1 tablespoon butter
60ml brandy

1 tablespoon soy sauce
1 teaspoon cranberry sauce
480ml chicken stock

1 teaspoon Worcestershire sauce

Preparation:

1. Switch the temperature of the Air fryer to 175°C. 2. In a bowl, merge salt, sweet paprika, black pepper, thyme, herbs, and garlic powder. 3. Rub oil over turkey and dredge in the seasoning. 4. Position the turkey in the Air fryer basket and air fry for about 40 minutes, flipping once in between. 5. Dish out and rest for 30 minutes. 6. Make the gravy In a saucepan, put butter and flour and cook for about 5 minutes on low heat to make a paste. 7. Whisk in brandy and stock and mix well. 8. Stir in all the sauces and simmer for 5 minutes until the sauce is thickened. 9. Dish out in a bowl and serve with turkey.

Serving Suggestions: Serve with crispy chips.

Variation Tip: You can also use almond flour instead of plain flour.

Nutritional Information per Serving:

Calories: 440 | Fat: 9g | Sat Fat: 3g | Carbohydrates: 5g | Fibre: 1g | Sugar: 1g | Protein: 77g

Buttered Herbed Turkey Thighs

Prep Time: 5 minutes | Cooking Time: 30 minutes | Servings: 4

Ingredients:

2 tablespoons light olive oil
2 turkey thighs, skin on and bone in
¼ teaspoon garlic powder

¼ teaspoon black pepper
1 tablespoon butter, melted
¼ teaspoon salt

¼ teaspoon Herbs de Provence

Preparation:

1. Switch the temperature of the Air fryer to 185°C. 2. In a bowl, merge olive oil and all of the seasonings. 3. Rub the seasoned oil on the turkey thighs. 4. Layer the turkey thighs in the Air fryer basket and air fry for about 30 minutes, flipping once in between. 5. Dish out and brush with melted butter to serve.

Serving Suggestions: Serve with cream cheese.

Variation Tip: You can add ginger powder too.

Nutritional Information per Serving:

Calories: 176 | Fat: 15.9g | Sat Fat: 2.8g | Carbohydrates: 0.2g | Fibre: 0.1g | Sugar: 0g | Protein: 9.1g

Turkey Crown with Orange

Prep Time: 5 minutes | Cooking Time: 50 minutes | Servings: 4

Ingredients:

2 teaspoons vegetable oil
1.35kg turkey crown

1 teaspoon sea salt
3 garlic cloves, mashed

1 orange, quartered
2 rosemary sprigs

Preparation:

1. Switch the temperature of the Air fryer to 175°C. 2. Rub the oil and salt onto the turkey crown. 3. Position the turkey crown on the Air fryer basket and arrange the orange quarters, garlic cloves, and rosemary on the side. 4. Air fry for about 50 minutes, flipping twice in between. 5. Dish out and serve after resting for 20 minutes.
Serving Suggestions: Serve with roasted veggies
Variation Tip: You can use butter instead of vegetable oil!
Nutritional Information per Serving:
Calories: 394 | Fat: 15g | Sat Fat: 4g | Carbohydrates: 5g | Fibre: 1g | Sugar: 3g | Protein: 58g

Herbed Garlic Turkey Thighs

Prep Time: 10 minutes | Cooking Time: 50 minutes | Servings: 4

Ingredients:

1 tablespoon olive oil
900g turkey thighs
½ teaspoon sea salt

1 tablespoon fresh basil, chopped
4 garlic cloves, peeled and coarsely chopped

½ teaspoon black pepper
1 tablespoon fresh parsley, chopped

Preparation:

1. Switch the temperature of the Air fryer to 175°C. 2. In a bowl, merge sea salt, black pepper, basil and thyme. 3. Rub the oil and seasonings on the turkey thighs. 4. Tuck garlic under the turkey skin and over it. 5. Layer the turkey thighs in the Air fryer basket and air fry for about 50 minutes, flipping once in between. 6. Dish out and serve hot.
Serving Suggestions: Serve with orange wedges and pomegranate arils.
Variation Tip: You can also make chicken breast with this recipe.
Nutritional Information per Serving:
Calories: 404 | Fat: 11g | Sat Fat: 1.7g | Carbohydrates: 3.2g | Fibre: 0.5g | Sugar: 0.2g | Protein: 73.9g

Buttered Herb Turkey Breast

Prep Time: 10 minutes | Cooking Time: 40 minutes | Servings: 6

Ingredients:

900g turkey breast, skin on
4 tablespoons butter, melted

Salt and black pepper, to taste
3 garlic cloves, crushed

1 teaspoon rosemary, freshly chopped
1 teaspoon thyme, freshly chopped

Preparation:

1. Switch the temperature of the Air fryer to 195°C. 2. In a bowl, merge melted butter, garlic, thyme, and rosemary. 3. Rub butter mixture over turkey breast and dust with salt and black pepper. 4. Position the turkey in the Air fryer basket and air fry for about 40 minutes, flipping once in between. 5. Dish out and serve warm.
Serving Suggestions: Serve with roasted garlic and onions.
Variation Tip: You can use herbs of your choice.
Nutritional Information per Serving:
Calories: 229 | Fat: 10.2g | Sat Fat: 5.4g | Carbohydrates: 7.1g | Fibre: 1g | Sugar: 5.3g | Protein: 26g

Homemade Turkey Burgers

Prep Time: 10 minutes | Cooking Time: 15 minutes | Servings: 4

Ingredients:

6 tortilla chips, crushed
455g turkey breast mince, uncooked
95g salsa

2 tablespoons spring onions, finely chopped
¼ teaspoon table salt
10g coriander, chopped

1 teaspoon ground cumin
¼ teaspoon black pepper
4 light hamburger bun

Preparation:

1. Switch the temperature of the Air fryer to 175°C. 2. In a bowl, merge all the ingredients except bun. 3. Thoroughly mix and form 1 cm-thick patties from this mixture. 4. Position the patties in the Air fryer basket and air fry for about 15 minutes, flipping once in between. 5. Dish out and serve warm inside buns.

Serving Suggestions: Serve with French fries.

Variation Tip: You can also use rolls instead of buns.

Nutritional Information per Serving:

Calories: 382 | Fat: 10.1g | Sat Fat: 2.6g | Carbohydrates: 37g | Fibre: 7.8g | Sugar: 4.1g | Protein: 39.1g

Herbed Garlic Duck Breast

Prep Time: 20 minutes | Cooking Time: 55 minutes | Servings: 4

Ingredients:

1 (1.35kg) duck breast
1 tablespoon fresh rosemary leaves, chopped
1 teaspoon lemon zest, finely grated

2 teaspoons salt, divided
3 tablespoons unsalted butter
1 tablespoon fresh thyme leaves
1 tablespoon fresh sage leaves, chopped

2 cloves garlic
1 teaspoon black pepper, divided

Preparation:

1. Switch the temperature of the Air fryer to 175°C. 2. In a bowl, merge butter, rosemary leaves, sage leaves, thyme leaves, lemon zest, garlic cloves, 1 teaspoon salt and ½ teaspoon black pepper to make a paste. 3. Stuff this mixture inside the duck breast skin and dust with salt and black pepper. 4. Position the duck skin side up in the Air fryer basket and air fry for about 55 minutes, flipping once in between. 5. Dish out and serve warm.

Serving Suggestions: Serve with stir fried veggies.

Variation Tip: You can make this recipe with chicken or turkey breasts too.

Nutritional Information per Serving:

Calories: 525 | Fat: 22.5g | Sat Fat: 5.6g | Carbohydrates: 2.2g | Fibre: 1g | Sugar: 0.1g | Protein: 75.3g

Herbed Turkey Legs

Prep Time: 10 minutes | Cooking Time: 40 minutes | Servings: 4

Ingredients:

1 teaspoon salt
4 turkey legs
1 teaspoon pepper

¼ teaspoon rosemary
¼ teaspoon thyme
1 tablespoon butter

¼ teaspoon oregano

Preparation:

1. Switch the temperature of the Air fryer to 175°C. 2. Dust the turkey legs with salt and black pepper. 3. In a bowl, merge butter with seasonings. 4. Rub butter mixture over and under the turkey legs. 5. Layer the turkey legs in the Air fryer basket and air fry for 40 minutes, flipping once in between. 6. Dish out and serve warm.

Serving Suggestions: Serve with Yorkshire pudding.

Variation Tip: You can also use olive oil instead of butter.

Nutritional Information per Serving:

Calories: 175 | Fat: 9.9g | Sat Fat: 4g | Carbohydrates: 0.5g | Fibre: 0.2g | Sugar: 0g | Protein: 19.9g

Spicy Turkey Tenderloin

Prep Time: 5 minutes | Cooking Time: 25 minutes | Servings: 2

Ingredients:

½ teaspoon thyme
1 turkey breast tenderloin

½ teaspoon black pepper
½ teaspoon pink salt

½ teaspoon paprika
½ teaspoon sage

Preparation:

1. Switch the temperature of the Air fryer to 175°C. 2. In a bowl, merge all the herbs and seasonings. 3. Scrub the turkey with the seasoning mixture. 4. Layer the turkey tenderloin in the Air fryer basket and air fry for about 25 minutes, flipping once in between. 5. Dish out and serve warm.

Serving Suggestions: Serve with mashed potatoes and fried green beans.
Variation Tip: You can add ground nutmeg too.
Nutritional Information per Serving:
Calories: 184 | Fat: 2.3g | Sat Fat: 0g | Carbohydrates: 0.9g | Fibre: 0.5g | Sugar: 0.1g | Protein: 42.2g

Turkey Strips with Three Peppers

Prep Time: 25 minutes | Cooking Time: 30 minutes | Servings: 4

Ingredients:

1 each red, green and yellow pepper, thinly sliced
2 tablespoons olive oil
2 cloves garlic, minced

1 red onion, thinly sliced
4 tablespoons cooking sherry
½ tablespoon spoon cider vinegar
1 teaspoon cornflour

455g turkey breast, sliced into thin strips
Salt and black pepper, to taste

Preparation:

1. Switch the temperature of the Air fryer to 175°C. 2. Layer the turkey strips in the Air fryer basket and air fry for about 20 minutes, flipping once in between. 3. Dish out in a plate and add peppers, garlic, and onions inside the Air fryer basket. 4. Trickle with olive oil and air fry for about 5 minutes. 5. Move the peppers mixture and turkey strips into a pan. 6. Merge the sherry, vinegar, and corn flour and whisk inside the pan. 7. Cook for about 5 minutes and dust with salt and black pepper. 8. Dish out and serve warm.

Serving Suggestions: Serve with white rice.
Variation Tip: You can also use peppers of your choice.
Nutritional Information per Serving:
Calories: 224 | Fat: 9.1g | Sat Fat: 1.4g | Carbohydrates: 12.9g | Fibre: 2.7g | Sugar: 7.4g | Protein: 20.6g

Spicy Turkey Wings

Prep Time: 5 minutes | Cooking Time: 25 minutes | Servings: 2

Ingredients:

2 turkey wings
2 teaspoons cooking oil

1 teaspoon salt, divided
1 teaspoon garlic powder, divided

½ teaspoon pepper, divided
1 teaspoon paprika, divided

Preparation:

1. Switch the temperature of the Air fryer to 200°C. 2. In a bowl, merge all the seasonings. 3. Scrub the turkey wings with the seasoning mixture. 4. Layer the turkey wings in the Air fryer basket and air fry for about 25 minutes, flipping once in between. 5. Dish out and serve warm.

Serving Suggestions: Serve with tomato ketchup.
Variation Tip: You can also use cooking spray.
Nutritional Information per Serving:
Calories: 186 | Fat: 11g | Sat Fat: 3g | Carbohydrates: 4g | Fibre: 1g | Sugar: 0.3g | Protein: 18g

Cheese Turkey Ciabatta

Prep Time: 10 minutes | Cooking Time: 10 minutes | Servings: 4

Ingredients:

4 ciabatta rolls
225g turkey breast, sliced into strips
225g brie, thinly sliced

1 medium Granny Smith apple, thinly sliced
4 tablespoons strawberry jam

2 tablespoons butter, slightly melted

Preparation:

1. Switch the temperature of the Air fryer to 180°C. 2. Apply butter and jam on both sides of the Ciabatta rolls. 3. Add 3 turkey strips on one side of each roll, layer with apple slices and Brie. 4. Cover the other halves of the rolls and move into the Air fryer basket. 5. Air fry for about 10 minutes, flipping once in between. 6. Dish out and serve warm.

Serving Suggestions: Serve with coleslaw.
Variation Tip: You can also use any other variety of apples.
Nutritional Information per Serving:
Calories: 497 | Fat: 24.3g | Sat Fat: 13.7g | Carbohydrates: 43.8g | Fibre: 2.5g | Sugar: 8.1g | Protein: 24.8g

Air Fryer Whole Duck with Potato

Prep Time: 5 minutes | Cooking Time: 1 hour | Servings: 8

Ingredients:

455g potatoes
2.3kg whole duck

1 tablespoon olive oil
Salt and black pepper

1 tablespoon thyme

Preparation:

1. Switch the temperature of the Air fryer to 185°C. 2. Dust the duck with salt and black pepper. 3. Scrub the duck with olive oil and position it on the Air fryer basket. 4. Air fry for about 40 minutes, flipping once in between. Dish out 5. Dust the potatoes with thyme, salt, and black pepper. 6. Air fry the potatoes for about 5 minutes and add the duck again. 7. Air fry for about 15 minutes and dish out to serve warm.

Serving Suggestions: Serve with roasted carrots.
Variation Tip: You can also add some spices.
Nutritional Information per Serving:
Calories: 638 | Fat: 36.6g | Sat Fat: 10.5g | Carbohydrates: 10.4g | Fibre: 2.8g | Sugar: 0.9g | Protein: 66.9g

Marinated Juicy Duck Leg

Prep Time: 15 minutes | Cooking Time: 25 minutes | Servings: 2

Ingredients:

2 duck legs

For the Marinade
½ teaspoon fresh ginger
1 orange, juiced

1 teaspoon granulated garlic
1 teaspoon chili powder

4 tablespoons olive oil
Salt and black pepper, to taste

Preparation:

1. Switch the temperature of the Air fryer to 180°C. 2. In a bowl, merge all the marinade ingredients. 3. Scrub the duck legs with the marinade and refrigerate for about 3 hours. 4. Layer the duck legs in the Air fryer basket and air fry for about 25 minutes, flipping twice in between. 5. Dish out and serve warm.

Serving Suggestions: Serve with grilled potatoes and salad.
Variation Tip: You can add chili to increase spiciness.
Nutritional Information per Serving:
Calories: 427 | Fat: 32.8g | Sat Fat: 5.1g | Carbohydrates: 12.9g | Fibre: 2.9g | Sugar: 9.1g | Protein: 23.1g

Herbed Turkey Crown

Prep Time: 5 minutes | Cooking Time: 50 minutes | Servings: 8

Ingredients:

2.3kg stuffed turkey crown
2 teaspoons mixed herbs

Salt and black pepper, to taste
Olive oil spray

Preparation:

1. Switch the temperature of the Air fryer to 180°C. 2. Layer the turkey crown breast side down in the Air fryer basket and season with olive oil, salt, pepper, and half of the mixed herbs. 3. Air fry for about 25 minutes and flip the turkey crown. 4. Dust the turkey breast with mixed herbs, salt, and black pepper. 5. Air fry for another 25 minutes and dish out to serve warm.
Serving Suggestions: You can serve with carrots and peas.
Variation Tip: You can use herbs of your choice.
Nutritional Information per Serving:
Calories: 296 | Fat: 4.8g | Sat Fat: 1g | Carbohydrates: 12.1g | Fibre: 1.5g | Sugar: 10g | Protein: 48.4g

Easy Fried Duck Breast

Prep Time: 5 minutes | Cooking Time: 17 minutes | Servings: 2

Ingredients:

2 duck breasts, boneless

½ teaspoon salt

¼ teaspoon black pepper

Preparation:

1. Switch the temperature of the Air fryer to 175°C. 2. Carve the skin of the duck breast and dust with salt and black pepper. 3. Position the duck breast in the Air fryer basket and air fry for about 17 minutes, flipping once in between. 4. Dish out and serve warm.
Serving Suggestions: Serve with hoisin sauce or gravy.
Variation Tip: You can also add spices of your choice.
Nutritional Information per Serving:
Calories: 485 | Fat: 26g | Sat Fat: 7g | Carbohydrates: 0g | Fibre: 0g | Sugar: 0g | Protein: 59g

Honey Roast Duck with Thyme

Prep Time: 5 minutes | Cooking Time: 50 minutes | Servings: 6

Ingredients:

1.3kg whole duck
2 tablespoons honey

2 sprig thymes - leaves only
1 orange

4 sprig thymes, whole
Salt and black pepper, to taste

Preparation:

1. Switch the temperature of the Air fryer to 200°C. 2. Rub the orange juice inside the duck and put two sprigs of thyme and two orange halves. 3. Dust with salt and black pepper and position on the Air fryer basket. 4. Trickle the honey over the duck and top with thyme leaves. 5. Air fry for about 50 minutes, flipping once in between. 6. Dish out and serve warm.
Serving Suggestions: Serve with pomegranate arils and rocket leaves.
Variation Tip: You can also use maple syrup.
Nutritional Information per Serving:
Calories: 458 | Fat: 31.3g | Sat Fat: 8.4g | Carbohydrates: 13.3g | Fibre: 1.1g | Sugar: 10.8g | Protein: 29.5g

Chapter 6 Beef, Pork and Lamb Recipes

Easy Roast Steak

Prep Time: 2 minutes | Cooking Time: 12 minutes | Servings: 1

Ingredients:

200g steak, around 2.5cm thick
Olive oil

½ teaspoon salt
½ teaspoon black pepper

Preparation:

1. Switch the temperature of the Air fryer to 200°C. 2. Scrub the steak with oil, salt, and pepper. 3. Layer the steak in the Air fryer basket and cook for about 12 minutes, flipping once in between. 4. Dish out and serve warm.
Serving Suggestions: Serve topped with garlic butter.
Variation Tip: You can add more spices if desired.
Nutritional Information per Serving:
Calories: 474 | Fat: 32.1g | Sat Fat: 14.3g | Carbohydrates: 0.6g | Fibre: 0.3g | Sugar: 0.1g | Protein: 45.7g

Herb Roast Beef

Prep Time: 5 minutes | Cooking Time: 45 minutes | Servings: 4

Ingredients:

Seasoning
2 teaspoons coarse salt
½ teaspoon dried thyme

½ teaspoon dried rosemary
1 teaspoon black pepper

½ teaspoon garlic granules
½ teaspoon brown sugar

For the Roast Beef
3 tablespoons olive oil

1.1kg roasting beef joint

Preparation:

1. Switch the temperature of the Air fryer to 200°C. 2. Merge all the seasoning ingredients and scrub the beef with this seasoning mixture and oil. 3. Layer the beef in the Air fryer basket and air fry for about 45 minutes, flipping once in between. 4. Dish out and serve warm.
Serving Suggestions: Serve with pickled onions.
Variation Tip: You can also use mustard powder instead of brown sugar.
Nutritional Information per Serving:
Calories: 125 | Fat: 11g | Sat Fat: 2g | Carbohydrates: 2g | Fibre: 1g | Sugar: 1g | Protein: 4g

Buttered Steak Bites & Mushrooms

Prep Time: 10 minutes | Cooking Time: 13 minutes | Servings: 3

Ingredients:

200g mushrooms, halved
455g steaks, cut into 1 cm cubes
2 tablespoons butter, melted

½ teaspoon garlic powder
Cracked black pepper, to taste
Melted butter, for finishing

1 teaspoon Worcestershire sauce
Salt, to taste
Minced parsley, garnish

Preparation:

1. Switch the temperature of the Air fryer to 200°C. 2. Merge the steak cubes and mushrooms and rub melted butter over it. 3. Scrub the steak cubes and mushrooms with Worcestershire sauce, garlic powder, salt, and black pepper. 4. Layer the steak and mushrooms evenly in the Air fryer basket and air fry for about 13 minutes. 5. Dish out and serve garnished with parsley.
Serving Suggestions: Serve with beetroot salad.
Variation Tip: You can use any cut of steak, ribeye, sirloin, or tri-tip.
Nutritional Information per Serving:
Calories: 401 | Fat: 29g | Sat Fat: 14g | Carbohydrates: 3g | Fibre: 1g | Sugar: 1g | Protein: 32g

Beef Strips with Sweet & Sour Sauce

Prep Time: 20 minutes | Cooking Time: 25 minutes | Servings: 3

Ingredients:

255g corn flour, seasoned with ½ teaspoon each of salt and pepper
135g rump steak sliced into strips

2 Birdseye chilies
1 handful dried red chilies
3 garlic cloves

1 teaspoon vegetable oil

The Marinade
1 piece fresh ginger
½ tablespoon sesame oil

1 teaspoon sugar
2 tablespoons light soy sauce

1 egg

The Sauce
½ tablespoon dark soy sauce
3 tablespoons tomato ketchup

6 tablespoons Chinkiang black rice vinegar
4 tablespoons honey

Preparation:

1. Switch the temperature of the Air fryer to 160°C. 2. Position the garlic and chilies in the Air fryer basket and air fry for about 15 minutes. 3. Dish out and keep aside in a plate. 4. Merge all the sauce ingredients and set aside this sauce. 5. Merge all the marinade ingredients and scrub the beef with it. 6. Coat all the beef strips with the corn flour. 7. Switch the Air fryer's temperature to 200°C. 8. Layer the beef strips in the Air fryer basket and air fry for about 10 minutes, flipping once in between. 9. Dish out and serve warm with sauce and roasted garlic and chili.
Serving Suggestions: Serve over fried rice.
Variation Tip: You can use coconut aminos instead of soy sauce.
Nutritional Information per Serving:
Calories: 560 | Fat: 14.1g | Sat Fat: 3.8g | Carbohydrates: 90.9g | Fibre: 7.4g | Sugar: 27.5g | Protein: 18.6g

Herbed Venison and Onion Meatballs

Prep Time: 20 minutes | Cooking Time: 40 minutes | Servings: 6

Ingredients:

455g venison
225g venison liver
160g minced onion
2 teaspoons dried thyme

½ teaspoon nutmeg
480ml beef stock
225g bacon ends
80g oats, coarsely ground

1 teaspoon salt
1 tablespoon fresh sage, minced
3 tablespoons fresh parsley, chopped
Caul fat or very thin bacon

Preparation:

1. Switch the temperature of the Air fryer to 190°C. 2. Chop the bacon, venison, and liver into small chunks and freeze for an hour. 3. Merge the meat with the onions and grind well in a grinder. 4. Dish out in a bowl and merge with the oats, herbs, and spices. 5. Form orange-sized balls from this mixture. 6. Untie the caul fat gently into single layer and place meatballs on it. 7. Wrap the meatball completely with the caul. 8. Layer the meatballs in the Air fryer tray and air fry for about 40 minutes, basting with beef stock every 10 minutes. 9. Dish out and serve warm.
Serving Suggestions: Serve with mashed potatoes and peas.
Variation Tip: You can also use breadcrumbs instead of oats.
Nutritional Information per Serving:
Calories: 314 | Fat: 2g | Sat Fat: 2g | Carbohydrates: 22g | Fibre: 4g | Sugar: 1g | Protein: 39g

Air Fryer Beef Hamburgers

Prep Time: 15 minutes | Cooking Time: 8 minutes | Servings: 4

Ingredients:

½ teaspoon salt
455g lean beef mince

½ teaspoon black pepper
¼ teaspoon garlic powder

½ teaspoon onion powder
60g barbecue sauce

For Serving
4 hamburger buns

Preparation:

1. Switch the temperature of the Air fryer to 185°C. 2. Merge the beef mince with salt, pepper, onion powder, and garlic powder. 3. Shape into patties and brush them with the barbecue sauce. 4. Layer the patties in the Air fryer basket and air fry for about 12 minutes, flipping once in between. 5. Dish out and serve warm inside buns.
Serving Suggestions: Serve with ketchup or salsa.
Variation Tip: You can also use your favorite rolls for serving.
Nutritional Information per Serving:
Calories: 365 | Fat: 19g | Sat Fat: 7g | Carbohydrates: 22g | Fibre: 1g | Sugar: 3g | Protein: 25g

Roast Beef with Red Wine Gravy

Prep Time: 15 minutes | Cooking Time: 55 hour | Servings: 4

Ingredients:

Roast Beef
1 teaspoon olive oil

900g beef, corner cut

Sea salt

Gravy
360ml red wine
2 teaspoons flour

1 teaspoon redcurrant jelly
600ml beef stock

Preparation:

1. Switch the temperature of the Air fryer to 200°C. 2. Rub the meat with oil and sea salt. 3. Position the meat in the Air fryer basket and air fry for about 15 minutes. 4. Switch the Air fryer's temperature to 180°C. 5. Air fry for another 30 minutes and dish out. 6. Merge all the ingredients for gravy and simmer for about 10 minutes. 7. Serve the roast beef with the gravy.
Serving Suggestions: Serve with steamed broccoli.
Variation Tip: You can also use white wine.
Nutritional Information per Serving:
Calories: 528 | Fat: 15.6g | Sat Fat: 5.7g | Carbohydrates: 5.5g | Fibre: 0g | Sugar: 0.7g | Protein: 70.7g

Buttered Sirloin Steak

Prep Time: 10 minutes | Cooking Time: 18 minutes | Servings: 2

Ingredients:

2 teaspoons salt
2 sirloin steaks, 3.5cm thick

2 teaspoons black pepper
2 tablespoons butter, melted

Preparation:

1. Switch the temperature of the Air fryer to 200°C. 2. Dust the steaks with salt and pepper, and scrub with the melted butter. 3. Layer the steak in the Air fryer basket and air fry for about 18 minutes, flipping once in between. 4. Dish out and serve warm.
Serving Suggestions: Serve with roasted asparagus.
Variation Tip: You can also serve with your favorite sauce.
Nutritional Information per Serving:
Calories: 265 | Fat: 16.9g | Sat Fat: 9.3g | Carbohydrates: 1.4g | Fibre: 0.6g | Sugar: 0g | Protein: 26.2g

Simple Air Fryer Sausages

Prep Time: 2 minutes | Cooking Time: 15 minutes | Servings: 6

Ingredients:

6 sausages

Preparation:

1. Switch the temperature of the Air fryer to 180°C. 2. Perforate the sausages all over with a knife 3. Layer the sausages in the Air fryer basket and air fry for about 15 minutes, flipping once in between. 4. Dish out and serve warm.
Serving Suggestions: You can serve with cauliflower cheese.
Variation Tip: You can use any kind of sausages for this recipe.
Nutritional Information per Serving:
Calories: 120 | Fat: 9g | Sat Fat: 3g | Carbohydrates: 4g | Fibre: 1g | Sugar: 1g | Protein: 6g

Easy Pigs in Blankets

Prep Time: 5 minutes | Cooking Time: 12 minutes | Servings: 4

Ingredients:

8 cocktail sausages
8 rashers smoked streaky bacon

Preparation:

1. Switch the temperature of the Air fryer to 180°C. 2. Wrap each cocktail sausage with one bacon rasher. 3. Layer the food in the Air fryer basket and air fry for about 12 minutes, flipping once in between. 4. Dish out and serve warm.
Serving Suggestions: Serve with Yorkshire Pudding.
Variation Tip: You can also use unsmoked streaky bacon.
Nutritional Information per Serving:
Calories: 314 | Fat: 24g | Sat Fat: 9g | Carbohydrates: 6g | Fibre: 1g | Sugar: 1g | Protein: 18g

Roast Lamb Legs with Potatoes

Prep Time: 15 minutes | Cooking Time: 40 minutes | Servings: 8

Ingredients:

1 large (1kg) leg of lamb
1 bunch oregano
6 tablespoons olive oil
1.35kg potatoes

1 large handful baby Kalamata olives, pitted
6 garlic cloves
1 lemon, zest and juice

300g tomatoes, chopped
A pinch of salt

Preparation:

1. Switch the temperature of the Air fryer to 200°C. 2. Merge garlic, half the oregano, lemon zest and a pinch of salt and pound them in a pestle and mortar. 3. Whisk in the lemon juice and olive oil. 4. Cut slits in the lamb and generously coat with the herb mixture. 5. Position the lamb in the Air fryer basket and add potatoes. 6. Air fry for about 40 minutes, flipping once in between. 7. Dish out and serve warm.
Serving Suggestions: Serve with carrots in addition to potatoes.
Variation Tip: You can increase the quantity of hot sauce for more spiciness.
Nutritional Information per Serving:
Calories: 685 | Fat: 36g | Sat Fat: 14g | Carbohydrates: 32g | Fibre: 3g | Sugar: 4g | Protein: 59g

Pork Pies with Piccalilli

Prep Time: 50 minutes | Cooking Time: 38 minutes | Servings: 12

Ingredients:

570g short-crust pastry, homemade
3 tablespoons butter
Little flour, for dusting
455g Cumberland sausage

¼ teaspoon each ground pepper, ground mace, and dried sage
1 teaspoon sesame seeds
75g dried white breadcrumb

110g smoked bacon lardon
1 egg, beaten
Piccalilli, to serve

Preparation:

1. Switch the temperature of the Air fryer to 200°C. 2. On a lightly floured board, roll out two-thirds of the pastry and cut out small circles. 3. Fill the bottom of each pie with 1 teaspoon of breadcrumbs. 4. Merge the remaining crumbs with sausage meat, bacon, mace, pepper, sage, and salt. 5. Thoroughly mix and divide this mixture into the pies. 6. Cut the remaining pastry into 12 x 7cm circles and brush with egg. 7. Top these circles with these pastries, egg side down. 8. Layer them in the Air fryer basket and air fry for about 30 minutes. 9. Dish out and serve warm.

Serving Suggestions: Serve with piccalilli or your favorite pickle.

Nutritional Information per Serving:

Calories: 373 | Fat: 25.1g | Sat Fat: 5.8g | Carbohydrates: 29.7g | Fibre: 1.5g | Sugar: 1.3g | Protein: 7.5g

British Herbed Toad in The Hole

Prep Time: 10 minutes | Cooking Time: 35 minutes | Servings: 4

Ingredients:

3 eggs
190g plain flour
600ml milk

2 tablespoons vegetable oil
8 sage leaves
2 teaspoons Dijon mustard

8 Cumberland sausages
4 rosemary sprigs
Salt and black pepper, to taste

Preparation:

1. Switch the temperature of the Air fryer to 200°C. 2. In a food processor, merge the eggs, flour, milk, mustard, salt and pepper until smooth. 3. Layer the sausages in the Air fryer tray, spray with oil and air fry for about 5 minutes, flipping once in between. 4. Whisk in the egg mixture and top with the sage leaves and rosemary. 5. Air fry for about 30 minutes and dish out to serve warm.

Serving Suggestions: Serve with roasted broccoli.

Variation Tip: You can also use almond flour.

Nutritional Information per Serving:

Calories: 552 | Fat: 32g | Sat Fat: 10g | Carbohydrates: 40g | Fibre: 1g | Sugar: 1.2g | Protein: 28g

Beef Roast with Caramelized Onion Gravy

Prep Time: 30 minutes | Cooking Time: 60 minutes | Servings: 6

Ingredients:

1 tablespoon English mustard powder
1 tablespoon black peppercorn
1 tablespoon dried thyme

1 tablespoon olive oil
1 teaspoon celery seeds
1.8kg topside joint of beef

Salt, to taste

For the Gravy
2 beef stock cubes
4 tablespoons plain flour

3 tablespoons caramelized onion chutney
3 teaspoons yeast extract

Preparation:

1. Switch the temperature of the Air fryer to 195°C. 2. Merge peppercorns, mustard powder, thyme and celery seeds together with some salt and pound them in a pestle and mortar. 3. Add oil and rub the meat with this mixture. 4. Position the meat in the Air fryer basket and air fry for about 20 minutes. 5. Switch the Air fryer's temperature to 180°C. 6. Air fry for another 30 minutes and dish out. 7. Merge all the ingredients for gravy and simmer for about 10 minutes. 8. Serve the roast beef with the gravy.

Serving Suggestions: Sprinkle with chives.

Variation Tip: You can use coconut flour.

Nutritional Information per Serving:

Calories: 591 | Fat: 28g | Sat Fat: 11g | Carbohydrates: 13g | Fibre: 1g | Sugar: 3g | Protein: 72g

Roast Lamb with Carrots Gravy

Prep Time: 10 minutes | Cooking Time: 1 hour 15 minutes | Servings: 4

Ingredients:

For the Lamb

2 onions, cut into chunks
5 carrots, cut into chunks
4 bay leaves

2 tablespoons olive oil
3 garlic cloves, thickly sliced, plus a whole
bulb, halved

1 small bunch rosemary
2.7kg large leg of lamb

For the Gravy

240ml white wine

5 tablespoons plain flour

720ml lamb stock

Preparation:

1. Switch the temperature of the Air fryer to 160°C. 2. For the lamb: In the Air fryer baking tray, merge vegetables, bay leaves, and rosemary sprigs, and trickle with olive oil. 3. Carve slits in the lamb and insert garlic slices and rosemary sprigs. 4. Position the lamb over the vegetables and put the baking tray inside the Air fryer. 5. Air fry for about 55 minutes, flipping once in between. 6. For the gravy: Put the Air fried vegetables in a deep pan along with the meat juices. 7. Cook well until the veggies are caramelized and then, add flour while constantly stirring. 8. Whisk in the wine and cook for 1 minute. 9. Add lamb stock and simmer for about 15 minutes to form a delicious gravy. 10. Dish out the lamb and serve drizzled with gravy.

Serving Suggestions: Serve over cooked rice.

Variation Tip: You can substitute coconut aminos with soy sauce.

Nutritional Information per Serving:

Calories: 532 | Fat: 30g | Sat Fat: 12g | Carbohydrates: 18g | Fibre: 2g | Sugar: 1.3g | Protein: 45g

Pork Cassoulet with Beans and Carrots

Prep Time: 30 minutes | Cooking Time: 1 hour | Servings: 8

Ingredients:

1 tablespoon sunflower oil
455g pork belly strips, rind trimmed
455g pack of pork sausages
2 cans cannellini, haricot, butter or mixed
beans, drained

4 medium carrots, thickly sliced
1 bouquet garni 'tea bag'
3 tablespoons fresh white breadcrumbs
4 back bacon chops
1 large onion, chopped

2 cans tomatoes, chopped
240ml chicken stock, boiled
2 garlic cloves

Preparation:

1. Switch the temperature of the Air fryer to 180°C. 2. Stir-fry the pork strips, sausages, and bacon chops in oil in a pan until browned. 3. In a bowl, merge onion, beans, garlic, carrots, and tomatoes. 4. Layer half the vegetables in the baking tray, followed by half the meat layer. 5. Repeat layering with the other halves of the vegetables and meats, and arrange bouquet garni in the centre. 6. Add chicken stock carefully and top with breadcrumbs. 7. Place the baking tray inside the Air fryer and air fry for about 1 hour. 8. Dish out and pour some more stock over the top to moisten before serving.

Serving Suggestions: Serve with macaroni.

Variation Tip: You can use pork rinds instead of breadcrumbs.

Nutritional Information per Serving:

Calories: 678 | Fat: 54.9g | Sat Fat: 18.7g | Carbohydrates: 14.3g | Fibre: 4.4g | Sugar: 4.4g | Protein: 30.4g

Tasty Shepherd's Pie

Prep Time: 15 minutes | Cooking Time: 1 hour 15 minutes | Servings: 4

Ingredients:

1 large onion, chopped
1 tablespoon sunflower oil
3 medium carrots, chopped
2 tablespoons tomato purée

480ml beef stock
185g butter
455g pack lamb mince
1 large splash Worcestershire sauce

900g. potatoes, cut into chunks and boiled
3 tablespoons milk

Preparation:

1. Switch the temperature of the Air fryer to 200°C. 2. In a saucepan, cook onions and carrots in sunflower oil for 5 minutes. 3. Add lamb mince, tomato purée and Worcestershire sauce. Cook for about 8 minutes. 4. Stir in the beef stock and cook for 40 minutes 5. Mash the potatoes with butter and milk. 6. In the Air fryer baking pan, add the mince and top with the potato mash. 7. Place in the Air fryer and air fry for about 20 minutes. 8. Dish out and serve warm.

Serving Suggestions: Serve with mashed potatoes.
Variation Tip: You can also use butter instead of oil.
Nutritional Information per Serving:
Calories: 663 | Fat: 39g | Sat Fat: 20g | Carbohydrates: 49g | Fibre: 5g | Sugar: 10g | Protein: 33g

Roast Beef Crostini

Prep Time: 20 minutes | Cooking Time: 19 minutes | Servings: 8

Ingredients:

1 tablespoon olive oil
340g beef fillet, from the thin end
1 teaspoon English mustard powder
2 tablespoons snipped chives

225g stilton
1 baguette, sliced diagonally
720g crème fraîche
1 teaspoon creamed horseradish

20g rocket leaf
Salt and black pepper, to taste

Preparation:

1. Switch the temperature of the Air fryer to 180°C. 2. Scrub oil and mustard over beef, and dust with salt and black pepper. 3. Sear the beef in a pan for about 4 minutes, turning once in between. 4. Layer the beef in the Air fryer basket and air fry for about 15 minutes. 5. In a bowl, merge crème fraîche, horseradish, chives, salt, and black pepper. 6. Dish out the beef in a platter along with the rocket, Stilton, and crème fraiche. 7. Toast the baguette slices and top with rocket, beef slices, cheese chunks, and crème fraiche dollops.

Serving Suggestions: Serve with chili garlic sauce.
Variation Tip: You can add red chili flakes for added spiciness.
Nutritional Information per Serving:
Calories: 497 | Fat: 34g | Sat Fat: 20g | Carbohydrates: 18g | Fibre: 1g | Sugar: 3g | Protein: 30g

Pork Steaks in Apple Mustard Sauce

Prep Time: 5 minutes | Cooking Time: 25 minutes | Servings: 4

Ingredients:

4 pork steaks, excess fat trimmed
1 tablespoon oil
2 apples, cored and chopped

1 onion, halved and sliced
2 teaspoons dried sage leaves
100ml chicken stock

2 teaspoons Dijon mustard
Salt and black pepper, to taste

Preparation:

1. Switch the temperature of the Air fryer to 200°C. 2. Rub oil over pork steaks and dust with salt and pepper. 3. Layer the pork steaks in the Air fryer basket and air fry for about 10 minutes. 4. Meanwhile, in a pan, cook the onions, apples, and sage for about 5 minutes in a little oil. 5. Stir in the stock and mustard, then add air fried pork steaks. 6. Simmer for about 10 minutes and dish out to serve.

Serving Suggestions: Serve with veggies and mashed potatoes.
Variation Tip: You can also use ham stock instead of chicken stock.
Nutritional Information per Serving:
Calories: 248 | Fat: 8g | Sat Fat: 2g | Carbohydrates: 9g | Fibre: 2g | Sugar: 8g | Protein: 35g

Herb-Roasted Lamb

Prep Time: 5 minutes | Cooking Time: 25 minutes | Servings: 2

Ingredients:

1 tablespoon olive oil
250g butterflied lamb leg roast

1 teaspoon rosemary, fresh or dried
½ teaspoon black pepper

A pinch of salt, to taste
1 teaspoon thyme, fresh or dried

Preparation:

1. Switch the temperature of the Air fryer to 180°C. 2. Rub olive oil, salt, black pepper, rosemary, and thyme over lamb roast. 3. Layer the lamb roast in the Air fryer basket and air fry for about 25 minutes. 4. Dish out in a platter and wait for 5 minutes to let the juices be absorbed before serving.

Serving Suggestions: Serve over egg fried rice.

Variation Tip: You can also add oregano for varied taste.

Nutritional Information per Serving:

Calories: 181 | Fat: 11g | Sat Fat: 2g | Carbohydrates: 1g | Fibre: 0g | Sugar: 0g | Protein: 18g

Beef, Vegetables with Noodles

Prep Time: 15 minutes | Cooking Time: 34 minutes | Servings: 6

Ingredients:

2 tablespoons sesame oil, toasted
570g rump steak, cut 1.5cm thick

500g stir fry vegetables
1 fine egg noodles, cooked

6 tablespoons hoisin sauce

Preparation:

1. Switch the temperature of the Air fryer to 200°C. 2. Scrub the beef with oil. 3. Layer the beef in the Air fryer basket and air fry for about 25 minutes, flipping once in between. 4. Add stir fry vegetables and air fry for another 5 minutes. 5. Dish out and transfer into a wok. 6. Whisk hoisin sauce with 2 tablespoons of water and add gently into the wok, continuously stirring. 7. Cook for 4 minutes and add in the egg noodles. 8. Mix thoroughly and dish out to serve warm.

Serving Suggestions: Serve with pickled vegetables.

Variation Tip: You can use any vegetables of your choice.

Nutritional Information per Serving:

Calories: 314 | Fat: 11.2g | Sat Fat: 0.9g | Carbohydrates: 20.7g | Fibre: 2.1g | Sugar: 6g | Protein: 32.5g

Chapter 7 Dessert Recipes

Scottish Dundee Cake

Prep Time: 35 minutes | Cooking Time: 45 minutes | Servings: 6

Ingredients:

145g blanched almonds
160g light sugar
170g softened unsalted butter,
zest of 1 large orange

155g plain flour
1 teaspoon baking powder
3 tablespoons apricot jam
3 large eggs, beaten

2 tablespoons milk
290g mixed dried fruit
95g ground almonds
120g whole glacé cherry

Glaze

1 tablespoon milk

2 teaspoons caster sugar

Preparation:

1. Switch the air fryer to 180°C. 2. Grease a baking pan that fits in the air fryer and line it with parchment paper. 3. Beat butter and sugar until fluffy. Add eggs, jam, orange zest, flour, and baking powder. Mix with the wooden spoon until well combined. 4. Stir in the ground almonds, milk, dried fruits, and cherries. 5. Pour the batter into the pan and level from the top. Arrange the blanched almonds on the top 6. Bake in the air fryer for 45 minutes. Check the cake by inserting the toothpick; remove it from the air fryer if it comes clean.

Serving Suggestions: Serve with butter and maple syrup.
Variation Tip: You can use apricot marmalade as well.
Nutritional Information per Serving:
Calories: 373 | Fat: 17.2g | Sat Fat: 6.7g | Carbohydrates: 48.4g | Fibre: 2.2g | Sugar: 38.6g | Protein: 6.3g

Apple Cake

Prep Time: 15minutes | Cooking Time: 45 minutes | Servings: 6

Ingredients:

125g flour
75g brown sugar
1 teaspoon ground nutmeg
1 teaspoon ground cinnamon

½ teaspoon baking soda
Salt, to taste
1 egg
5 tablespoons plus 1 teaspoon of vegetable

oil
¾ teaspoon vanilla extract
220g apples, peeled, cored, and chopped

Preparation:

1. Mix flour, sugar, spices, baking soda, and salt in a bowl. 2. In another bowl, add the egg and oil and whisk until smooth. 3. Add the vanilla extract and whisk well. 4. Slowly add the flour mixture, whisking continuously until well combined. 5. Fold in the chopped apples. 6. Switch the air fryer to 180°C. Lightly grease a cake pan. 7. Place the mixture evenly into the prepared cake pan. 8. Cover the pan with a piece of foil and poke some holes using a fork. 9. Arrange the cake pan into an air fryer basket. 10. Now, switch the temperature of the air fryer to 160°C. 11. Air fry for about 40 minutes. 12. Remove the foil and air fry for another 5 minutes. 13. Remove the cake pan from the air fryer and let it cool for 10 minutes. 14. Now, invert the cake onto a wire rack to cool completely before slicing. 15. Cut the cake into desired size slices and serve.

Serving Suggestions: Serve with icing sugar on top.
Variation Tip: You can add apple extract for more taste variation.
Nutritional Information per Serving:
Calories: 260 | Fat: 12.5g | Sat Fat: 3g | Carbohydrates: 34.7g | Fibre: 5g | Sugar: 34.5g | Protein: 3.3g

Homemade Welsh Cakes

Prep Time: 10 minutes | Cooking Time: 6 minutes | Servings: 4

Ingredients:

125g plain flour
55g butter, cut into small pieces
½ teaspoon mixed spice
100g caster sugar

½ teaspoon baking powder
35g currants
50g lard, cut into small pieces
Oil for spraying

1 egg, beaten
Splash of milk

Preparation:

1. Mix flour, mixed spice, sugar, currants, and mixed spice together. Add butter and lard to the flour and mix with the hand until the mixture is crumbly. 2. Knead the mixture by adding egg and a splash of milk. 3. Roll out the dough 2.5cm of thickness. Cut circles with the cookie dough. Re-roll the dough and cut circles until you consume all the dough. 4. Switch the air fryer to 175°C. spray the welsh cakes with oil on both sides and place them in the air fryer in a single layer. 5. Cook for 6 minutes in total. Flip the cakes after the first three minutes. 6. Remove once brown from both sides. 7. Cook the rest in batches repeating the same steps.

Serving Suggestions: Serve with English tea.

Variation Tip: You can only use vegetable shortening instead of lard.

Nutritional Information per Serving:

Calories: 138 | Fat: 6g | Sat Fat: 1g | Carbohydrates: 20g | Fibre: 9g | Sugar: 9g | Protein: 2g

Lemon Spotted Dick

Prep Time: 15 minutes | Cooking Time: 30 minutes | Servings: 6

Ingredients:

220g self-rising flour
100g shredded suet
Pinch of salt
100g caster sugar

145g currant
Finely grated zest of 1 lemon
180ml whole milk, plus 2-3 tablespoons
Finely grated zest of 1 small orange

Oil or butter for greasing
Custard, to serve

Preparation:

1. Add flour, suet, salt, and sugar in a mixing bowl. Add sugar, lemon, and orange zest and mix well. 2. Pour milk and knead. It should form a moist dough. Add a dash of milk if the dough is on the dry side. 3. Take 6 steel molds and grease them with butter or oil. 4. Divide the dough and push in the molds. Leave about 1 cm from the top. 5. Cover the cups tightly with foil paper 6. Pour some hot boiling water into the air fryer basket. Place the molds and air fry at 95°C for 30 minutes. 7. Dish out and serve.

Serving Suggestions: Serve with egg custard.

Variation Tip: You can also add lemon zest instead of orange zest.

Nutritional Information per Serving:

Calories: 462 | Fat: 19.9g | Sat Fat: 11.2g | Carbohydrates: 65g | Fibre: 2.7g | Sugar: 34.5g | Protein: 5.4g

Quick and Easy Banoffee Pie

Prep Time: 5 minutes | Cooking Time: 3 minutes | Servings: 1

Ingredients:

20g crushed digestive biscuits
1 tablespoon melted butter, unsalted

1 banana, sliced
2 tablespoons caramel

whipped cream, sliced bananas, and
chocolate shavings, for Serving (Optional)

Preparation:

1. In a ramekin, add melted butter and then add biscuit crumbs and push with the back of the spoon 2. Add sliced bananas and drizzle caramel on top. 3. Switch the air fryer to 150°C and put the ramekin in the air fryer for 3 minutes 4. Serve with a dollop of cream and chocolate shavings.

Serving Suggestions: Serve with sliced bananas and walnuts

Variation Tip: You can also use dulce de leche

Nutritional Information per Serving:

Calories: 435 | Fat: 14.6g | Sat Fat: 7.5g | Carbohydrates: 77.1g | Fibre: 5.2g | Sugar: 19.8g | Protein: 3.8g

Classic Yorkshire Curd Tart

Prep Time: 45 minutes | Cooking Time: 40 minutes | Servings: 6

Ingredients:

For the Pastry
140g plain flour
pinch baking powder

6 tablespoons cold salted butter
1 teaspoon caster sugar

For the Filling
1.2L full-fat milk
2 tablespoons lemon juice

55g unsalted butter
50g caster sugar

1 large egg, beaten
35g currants

Preparation:

1. For the Curd Filling: Heat milk to a boiling point in a saucepan. Lower the heat and add lemon juice. Gently stir until the curd separates from the whey. Let it cool, and then strain the curd. Keep in a cheesecloth and set aside for 30 minutes. 2. Beat sugar and butter. Then add an egg. Beat till you get a smooth mixture. Then add curd and beat lightly. Finally, add currants and gently mix the filling with the spatula. 3. For the Pastry: In a food processor, mix all pastry ingredients and pulse till the mixture gets crumbly. Add a bit of cold water to get a sticky variety. Knead with hands and then keep it in the fridge for 20 minutes. 4. Assemble the tart by rolling the crust and placing it in a pie dish that fits in the air fryer. Spread the filling in the crust and air fry at 150°C for 40 minutes until the top is firm and brown.
Serving Suggestions: Serve with a drizzle of cream.
Variation Tip: You can use goat's cheese instead of curd.
Nutritional Information per Serving:
Calories: 466 | Fat: 30g | Sat Fat: 19g | Carbohydrates: 40g | Fibre: 1g | Sugar: 23g | Protein: 11g

Bread and Raisin Pudding

Prep Time: 20 minutes | Cooking Time: 20 minutes | Servings: 6

Ingredients:

240ml milk
1 egg
1 tablespoon brown sugar
½ teaspoon ground cinnamon

¼ teaspoon vanilla extract
2 tablespoons raisins, soaked in hot water
for about 15 minutes
2 bread slices, cut into small cubes

1 tablespoon chocolate chips
1 tablespoon sugar

Preparation:

1. Mix milk, egg, brown sugar, cinnamon, and vanilla extract well in a bowl. 2. Stir in the raisins. 3. In a baking dish, spread the bread cubes and top evenly with the milk mixture. 4. Refrigerate for about 15-20 minutes. 5. Switch the air fryer to 190°C. 6. Remove from refrigerator and sprinkle with chocolate chips and sugar on top. 7. Arrange the baking dish into an air fryer basket. 8. Air fry for about 12 minutes. 9. Once done, serve warm.
Serving Suggestions: You can serve with custard.
Variation Tip: You can use any bread.
Nutritional Information per Serving:
Calories: 143 | Fat: 4.4g | Sat Fat: 1.3g | Carbohydrates: 21.3g | Fibre: 1g | Sugar: 16.4g | Protein: 5.5g

Easy Apple Crumble

Prep Time: 10 minutes | Cooking Time: 25 minutes | Servings: 4

Ingredients:

1 (350g) can of apple pie filling
25g butter, softened

9 tablespoons self-rising flour
7 tablespoons caster sugar

Pinch of salt

Preparation:

1. Switch the air fryer to 160°C. Lightly grease a baking dish that fits the air fryer. 2. Place apple pie filling evenly into the prepared baking dish. 3. In a medium bowl, add the remaining ingredients and mix until a crumbly mixture forms. 4. Spread the mixture evenly over the apple pie filling. 5. Arrange the baking dish in the air fryer and air fry for about 25 minutes. 6. Once done, take it out of the air fryer and let it cool
Serving Suggestions: Serve with ice cream
Variation Tip: You can also use hazelnuts in the crumble mixture.
Nutritional Information per Serving:
Calories: 340 | Fat: 11.8g | Sat Fat: 1.1g | Carbohydrates: 60.3g | Fibre: 4.7g | Sugar: 34.8g | Protein: 2g

Mini Cinnamon Apple Pie

Prep Time: 20 minutes | Cooking Time: 30 minutes | Servings: 6

Ingredients:

For Crust

190g flour

1 teaspoon sugar

Salt, to taste

115g unsalted butter

60ml chilled water

For Filling

4 Granny Smith apples, peeled and finely chopped

1 teaspoon fresh lemon zest, finely grated

2½ tablespoons sugar

2 tablespoons flour

1 teaspoon ground cinnamon

¼ teaspoon ground nutmeg

Salt, to taste

75g Nutella

2 tablespoons fresh lemon juice

2 tablespoons butter

For Topping

1 egg, beaten

3 tablespoons sugar

1 teaspoon ground cinnamon

Preparation:

1. For the Crust: In a bowl, mix well flour, sugar, butter, and salt. Cut in the butter. Add the chilled water and mix until a dough forms. With a plastic wrapper, cover the bowl and refrigerate for about 30 minutes. 2. For the filling: Mix all the ingredients well in a large bowl. Set aside. 3. Now, place the dough onto a lightly floured surface and roll to 1 cm thickness. With a cookie cutter, cut 12 circles from the dough. 4. Place 6 circles in the bottom of 6 ramekins and press slightly. Add the filling mixture to the ramekins and top with the remaining circles. Pinch the edges to seal the pies. 5. Carefully cut 3 slits in each pie and coat evenly with the beaten egg. 6. For the topping, mix the cinnamon and sugar in a small bowl. 7. Sprinkle each pie with cinnamon sugar. 8. Switch the air fryer to 175°C. 9. Arrange the ramekins into an air fryer basket. Air fry for about 30 minutes. 10. Remove the ramekins from the air fryer and place them onto a wire rack to cool for about 10-15 minutes before serving. 11. Serve warm.

Serving Suggestions: Serve with whipped cream

Variation Tip: You can use a variety of ready-made crusts.

Nutritional Information per Serving:

Calories: 442 | Fat: 22.6g | Sat Fat: 2.3g | Carbohydrates: 58.2g | Fibre: 4g | Sugar: 29.6g | Protein: 5.2g

Homemade Sweet Potato Pie

Prep Time: 20 minutes | Cooking Time: 35 minutes | Servings: 6

Ingredients:

150g sweet potato

1 teaspoon olive oil

1 (24cm) prepared frozen pie dough, thawed

60g heavy cream

2 large eggs

2 tablespoons maple syrup

1 tablespoon butter, melted

1 tablespoon light brown sugar

½ teaspoon ground cinnamon

⅛ teaspoon ground nutmeg

Salt, to taste

¾ teaspoon vanilla extract

Preparation:

1. Switch the air fryer to 200°C and preheat for 10 minutes. 2. Coat the sweet potato evenly with oil. 3. Arrange the sweet potato into an air fryer basket. 4. Air fry for about 3 minutes. 5. Once done, remove it from the air fryer and let it cool completely. 6. Peel the sweet potato and mash it thoroughly. 7. Place the pie dough onto a floured surface and cut it into an 20 cm pie shell. 8. Arrange the dough shell into a greased pie pan. 9. Mix mashed sweet potato and remaining ingredients until well combined. 10. Place sweet potato mixture evenly over the pie shell. 11. Switch the temperature of the air fryer to 160°C. 12. Arrange the pie pan into an air fryer basket. 13. Air fry for about 30 minutes. Once cooked, take it out of the air fryer and let it cool for 10 minutes. 14. Serve warm.

Serving Suggestions: Serve with whipped cream.

Variation Tip: You can use almonds or pecans in the filling.

Nutritional Information per Serving:

Calories: 233 | Fat: 12.2g | Sat Fat: 1.3g | Carbohydrates: 27.8g | Fibre: 1.6g | Sugar: 16.6g | Protein: 3.8g

Simple Apple Pie

Prep Time: 15 minutes | Cooking Time: 30 minutes | Servings: 6

Ingredients:

1 frozen pie crust, thawed
1 large apple, peeled, cored and chopped
3 tablespoons sugar divided

1 tablespoon ground cinnamon
2 teaspoons fresh lemon juice
½ teaspoon vanilla extract

1 tablespoon butter, chopped
1 egg, beaten

Preparation:

1. Grease a pie pan. 2. With a smaller baking tin, cut one crust from thawed pie crust about ¼ cm larger than the pie pan. 3. Cut the second crust from the pie crust a little smaller than the first one. 4. Arrange the large crust in the bottom of the prepared pie pan. 5. Mix the apple, 2 tablespoons of sugar, cinnamon, lemon juice, and vanilla extract in a bowl. 6. Place apple mixture evenly over the bottom crust. 7. Add the chopped butter over the apple mixture. 8. Arrange the second crust on top and pinch the edges to seal. 9. Carefully cut 3-4 slits in the top crust. 10. Spread the beaten egg evenly over the top crust and sprinkle with the remaining sugar. 11. Switch the air fryer to 160°C. 12. Arrange the pie pan into an air fryer basket. 13. Air fry for about 30 minutes. 14. Let it cool for about 10-15 minutes before serving. 15. Serve warm.

Serving Suggestions: Serve with whipped cream.
Variation Tip: You can use mixed spices instead of cinnamon for a variation in taste.
Nutritional Information per Serving:
Calories: 190 | Fat: 3.1g | Sat Fat: 1.0g | Carbohydrates: 25.3g | Fibre: 3.1g | Sugar: 1.6g | Protein: 11.8g

Apple Cake with Walnut

Prep Time: 20 minutes | Cooking Time: 30 minutes | Servings: 8-10

Ingredients:

170g softened butter, plus extra for greasing
1 tsp vanilla extract
2 eggs
150g golden caster sugar

220g self-rising flour
½ teaspoon cinnamon
2 apples - peeled, cored and chopped in chunks

4 heaped tablespoons of Greek yogurt
30g of chopped walnuts
Icing sugar for dusting

Preparation:

1. Switch the air fryer to 150°C. 2. Grease a loaf pan that fits in the air fryer. 3. Beat sugar, butter, and vanilla with an electric beater. 4. Add eggs one at a time, and then add flour, yogurt, and cinnamon. 5. Fold apples in the cake mixture. 6. Pour the batter into the loaf pan and spread walnuts on the cake. 7. Place it in the air fryer for 30 minutes. Check by inserting the skewer. If it comes out clean, remove it from the air fryer. 8. Let it cool for 10 minutes. 9. Dust it with icing sugar. Slice and serve.

Serving Suggestions: Serve with English tea.
Variation Tip: You can also add raisins in the cake.
Nutritional Information per Serving:
Calories: 490 | Fat: 29g | Sat Fat: 15g | Carbohydrates: 53g | Fibre: 2g | Sugar: 30g | Protein: 7g

Custard Tart with Nutmeg

Prep Time: 10 minutes | Cooking Time: 30 minutes | Servings: 12

Ingredients:

275g sheet shortcrust pastry
4 egg yolks
120g double cream

1 tsp vanilla bean paste
120ml milk
½ a nutmeg

100g caster sugar

Preparation:

1. Switch the air fryer to 150°C. 2. Cut 12 circles from the pastry. 3. Gently press these circles in the cupcake tray and place it in the air fryer for 10 minutes. 4. For the custard, bring cream and milk to a boil. Add vanilla and nutmeg and remove from heat. 5. Beat egg yolks and sugar until pale in colour. Pour the hot cream mixture and beat thoroughly. 6. Strain the mixture and keep it aside for 5 minutes. 7. Fill each tart with the custard and grate some nutmeg on the top. 8. Place the tarts back in the air fryer and bake for 15 minutes until the filling is firm and slightly wobbly. 9. Remove and cool.

Serving Suggestions: Serve with grated nutmeg.
Variation Tip: You can also use puff pastry instead of short-crust pastry.
Nutritional Information per Serving:
Calories: 213 | Fat: 15g | Sat Fat: 9g | Carbohydrates: 16g | Fibre: 1g | Sugar: 5g | Protein: 3g

Oat Flapjacks

Prep Time: 15 minutes | Cooking Time: 20 minutes | Servings: 2

Ingredients:

180g jumbo porridge oats
115g butter, plus extra for the tin

105g light brown sugar
2-3 tablespoons golden syrup (depending

on how gooey you want it)

Preparation:

1. Switch the air fryer to 175°C. 2. Put the butter, sugar, oats and golden syrup in a mixing bowl and mix with a wooden spoon. 3. Grease a baking pan with butter and put the oat mixture in it. Press it from the back of the spoon and level the top. 4. Place it in the air fryer and bake for 20 minutes until golden brown. 5. Once cooked, cut the square flapjacks.
Serving Suggestions: Serve with Coffee.
Variation Tip: You can use a variety of nuts for taste variation.
Nutritional Information per Serving:
Calories: 212 | Fat: 10g | Sat Fat: 6g | Carbohydrates: 27g | Fibre: 2g | Sugar: 13g | Protein: 2g

Baked Manchester Tart

Prep Time: 25 minutes | Cooking Time: 25 minutes | Servings: 12

Ingredients:

275g ready-to-bake puff pastry
150g raspberry jam

45g desiccated coconut, lightly toasted
12 maraschino cherries

For the Custard
720ml whole milk
2 tsp vanilla bean paste

5 large egg yolks
100g caster sugar

4 tablespoons custard powder

For Icing
Whipping cream

Preparation:

1. Roll the pastry and cut circles from a cookie cutter. Place these circles in the tart molds. 2. Switch the air fryer to 150°C and place the tarts. Bake for 20 minutes. Remove once golden brown and set them aside. 3. For the custard, heat milk to the boiling point. Whisk egg yolks, sugar, vanilla, and custard powder. Pour hot milk over it, whisking continuously. 4. Place the custard on low heat and stir until the custard thickens. Once cooked, cool the custard slightly. 5. Assemble Manchester tarts by spreading jam in the base of the tarts, then fill it up with custard. 6. Pipe the whipping cream on the tarts, sprinkle desiccated coconut and top with cherries. 7. put it in the fridge for 30 minutes. 8. Serve cold.
Serving Suggestions: serve with hot tea.
Variation Tip: You can also use short-crust pastry for the base.
Nutritional Information per Serving:
Calories: 342 | Fat: 15g | Sat Fat: 9g | Carbohydrates: 46g | Fibre: 2g | Sugar: 29g | Protein: 6g

Victoria Sponge Cake

Prep Time: 20 minutes | Cooking Time: 20 minutes | Servings: 10

Ingredients:

230g unsalted butter, softened, plus extra
for greasing
100g caster sugar
1 teaspoon vanilla extract

4 medium eggs
190g self-rising flour, plus extra for dusting
6 tablespoons of raspberry jam
240g double cream, whipped

Icing sugar for dusting
Fresh fruits for topping

Preparation:

1. Switch to the air fryer to 200°C. 2. Grease the baking pan with butter. 3. In a stand mixer, cream together sugar and butter. Add eggs one by one and mix until combined well. Fold in the flour and stir well. 4. Pour the batter in the greased pan and bake in the air fryer for 20 minutes or until they are springy to the touch. 5. Let it cool for some time, and then remove from the baking pan. 6. Once cooled, divide the sponge into two. 7. Spread the jam onto the cake and top with the whipped cream. 8. Place the other half on top and dust it with icing sugar.
Serving Suggestions: You can serve with fresh fruits on top.
Variation Tip: You can use vanilla bean paste to enhance the flavor.
Nutritional Information per Serving:
Calories: 599 | Fat: 40g | Sat Fat: 23g | Carbohydrates: 56g | Fibre: 1g | Sugar: 38g | Protein: 6g

Rhubarb Muffins with Oats Crumble

Prep Time: 25 minutes | Cooking Time: 18 minutes | Servings: 12

Ingredients:

For the Muffin Mix

120g rhubarb, diced
175g caster sugar
2 tablespoons vegetable oil

1 teaspoon vanilla extract
1 egg
120ml buttermilk

120g plain flour
1 teaspoon bicarbonate of soda
1 teaspoon baking powder

For the Crumble Topping

30g plain flour
50g light muscovado sugar

1 teaspoon ground cinnamon
20g porridge oats

115g butter

Preparation:

1. Switch the air fryer to 200°C. Line a muffin pan with muffin liners and set aside. 2. In a bowl put, mix rhubarb and sugar and set aside. 3. Mix all the ingredients of the topping until a crumbly mixture forms. 4. Beat eggs, buttermilk, oil, and egg with an electric mixture. Mix sugary rhubarbs in the mixture. 5. Add flour, baking soda, and baking powder and mix well. Use a spatula for mixing; make sure not to overmix. 6. Scoop out the muffin mixture in the prepared muffin tray and spread a thick layer of the crumbled topping. 7. Bake in the air fryer for 18 minutes. Check by inserting a toothpick. If it comes out clean, remove it from the air fryer. 8. Let it cool, and then serve.

Serving Suggestions: Serve with cream cheese.

Variation Tip: you can also add ground nuts to the crumbled mixture.

Nutritional Information per Serving:

Calories: 213 | Fat: 6g | Sat Fat: 3g | Carbohydrates: 38g | Fibre: 1g | Sugar: 21g | Protein: 4g

Cherry Tart

Prep Time: 30 minutes | Cooking Time: 40 minutes | Servings: 12

Ingredients:

275g sheets of short crust pastry

For the Filling

50g of softened butter
50g of golden caster sugar

1 egg
1 tablespoon plain flour

50g ground almonds
25g cherry jam

For the Icing

60g icing sugar

Glazed cherries for topping

Preparation:

1. Switch the air fryer to 150°C. 2. Grease a muffin tin that fits in the air fryer 3. Spread the pastry and cut circles. Line these in the muffin molds. Push them down and fix them. 4. Chill it in the fridge for 10 minutes. Then bake it in the air fryer for 20 minutes until golden brown. Remove from the air fryer and let them cool. Remove from the mold and set it aside. 5. For the filling: Beat sugar with butter until light. Add up egg and flour. Fold almonds and jam in the mixture. 6. Fill the mixture in each shell. 7. Bake in the air fryer for another 20 minutes till the filling is firm and brown. 8. For the icing: Mix the icing sugar with a tablespoon of water and spread it on the tarts. 9. Put glazed cherries on top and serve.

Serving Suggestions: Serve with Tea.

Variation Tip: You can also use walnuts instead of almonds.

Nutritional Information per Serving:

Calories: 534 | Fat: 30g | Sat Fat: 12g | Carbohydrates: 57g | Fibre: 2g | Sugar: 32g | Protein: 6g

Easy Peach Cobbler

Prep Time: 25 minutes | Cooking Time: 30 minutes | Servings: 12

Ingredients:

350g can sliced peaches, drained
1 egg
½ tsp ground ginger
70g golden caster sugar, plus extra for

sprinkling
65g plain flour
¼ tsp ground cinnamon
1 tsp baking powder

75g butter, chilled and cubed, plus extra for
greasing
A pinch of salt
Icing sugar for dusting

Preparation

1. Switch the air fryer to 95°C and preheat for 10 minutes. 2. Grease a baking dish with butter. 3. Drain the peaches and place them in the dish. 4. Sprinkle 2 tablespoons of sugar and ginger on top and then set aside. 5. Mix flour, baking powder, remaining sugar, cinnamon, and a pinch of salt in a food processor. Add butter and pulse till you get a crumbly mixture. 6. Spoon the dollops of mixture over the peaches and cover them completely. 7. Bake in the air fryer for 30 minutes and remove once golden brown from the top. 8. Dust with icing sugar and serve warm.

Serving Suggestions: Serve with vanilla ice cream.

Variation Tip: You can use the same amount of self-rising flour instead of flour and baking powder.

Nutritional Information per Serving:

Calories: 648 | Fat: 32g | Sat Fat: 20g | Carbohydrates: 81g | Fibre: 3g | Sugar: 52g | Protein: 6g

Conclusion

The Air Fryer is an incredible kitchen appliance that can air fry, crisp, roast, bake, broil, reheat, and dehydrate meats and vegetables. With this appliance, you can have deliciously fried and baked food and healthier desserts and snacks. It eliminates extra fats from the food, and you can have it up to your desired level of crispiness. This all-in-one food appliance is perfect for anyone who wants to lighten their kitchen workload by taking care of all the frying and baking with just one appliance!

This appliance is perfect for those ready to switch to a healthy lifestyle and embark on their weight loss journey. With dishwasher-safe accessories and easy-to-understand cooking settings, it's ideal for cooking healthy meals for yourself and your loved ones. The high-capacity pot means you can cook for the whole family at once, instead of making multiple batches. So let's get cooking!

Appendix 1 Measurement Conversion Chart

WEIGHT EQUIVALENTS

US STANDARD	METRIC (APPROXIMATE)
1 ounce	28 g
2 ounces	57 g
5 ounces	142 g
10 ounces	284 g
15 ounces	425 g
16 ounces (1 pound)	455 g
1.5pounds	680 g
2pounds	907 g

TEMPERATURES EQUIVALENTS

FAHRENHEIT(F)	CELSIUS (C) (APPROXIMATE)
225 °F	107 °C
250 °F	120 °C
275 °F	135 °C
300 °F	150 °C
325 °F	160 °C
350 °F	180 °C
375 °F	190 °C
400 °F	205 °C
425 °F	220 °C
450 °F	235 °C
475 °F	245 °C
500 °F	260 °C

VOLUME EQUIVALENTS (DRY)

US STANDARD	METRIC (APPROXIMATE)
⅛ teaspoon	0.5 mL
¼ teaspoon	1 mL
½ teaspoon	2 mL
¾ teaspoon	4 mL
1 teaspoon	5 mL
1 tablespoon	15 mL
¼ cup	59 mL
½ cup	118 mL
¾ cup	177 mL
1 cup	235 mL
2 cups	475 mL
3 cups	700 mL
4 cups	1 L

VOLUME EQUIVALENTS (LIQUID)

US STANDARD	US STANDARD (OUNCES)	METRIC (APPROXIMATE)
2 tablespoons	1 fl.oz	30 mL
¼ cup	2 fl.oz	60 mL
½ cup	4 fl.oz	120 mL
1 cup	8 fl.oz	240 mL
1½ cup	12 fl.oz	355 mL
2 cups or 1 pint	16 fl.oz	475 mL
4 cups or 1 quart	32 fl.oz	1 L
1 gallon	128 fl.oz	4 L

Appendix 2 Air Fryer Cooking Chart

Vegetables	Temp(℉)	Time
Asparagus (1" slices)	400	5
Beets (whole)	400	40
Broccoli Florets	400	6
Brussel Sprouts (halved)	380	12-15
Carrots (1/2" slices)	360	12-15
Cauliflower Florets	400	10-12
Corn on the Cob	390	6-7
Eggplant (1 1/2" cubes)	400	12-15
Green Beans	400	4-6
Kale Leaves	250	12
Mushrooms (1/4" slices)	400	4-5
Onions (pearl)	400	10
Peppers (1" chunks)	380	8-15
Potatoes (whole)	400	30-40
Potatoes (wedges)	390	15-18
Potatoes (1" cubes)	390	12-15
Potatoes (baby, 1.5 lbs.)	400	15
Squash (1" cubes)	390	15
Sweet Potato (whole)	380	30-35
Tomatoes (cherry)	400	5
Zucchini (1/2" sticks)	400	10-12

Frozen Foods	Temp(℉)	Time
Breaded Shrimp	400	8-9
Chicken Burger	360	12
Chicken Nuggets	370	10-12
Chicken Strips	380	12-15
Corn Dogs	400	7-9
Fish Fillets (1-2 lbs.)	400	10-12
Fish Sticks	390	12-15
French Fries	380	12-17
Hash Brown Patties	380	10-12
Meatballs (1-inch)	350	10-12
Mozzarella Sticks (11 oz.)	400	8
Meat Pies (1-2 pies)	370	23-25
Mozzarella Sticks	390	7-9
Onion Rings	400	10-12
Pizza	390	5-10
Tater Tots	380	15-17

Beef	Temp(℉)	Time (min)
Burgers (1/4 Pound)	350	8-12
Filet Mignon (4 oz.)	370	15-20
Flank Steak (1.5 lbs)	400	10-14
Meatballs (1 inch)	380	7-10
London Broil (2.5 lbs.)	400	22-28
Round Roast (4 lbs)	390	45-55
Sirloin Steak (12oz)	390	9-14

Fish & Seafood	Temp(℉)	Time
Calamari	400	4-5
Fish Fillets	400	10-12
Salmon Fillets	350	8-12
Scallops	400	5-7
Shrimp	370	5-7
Lobster Tails	370	5-7
Tuna Steaks	400	7-10

Chicken	Temp(℉)	Time(min)
Chicken Whole (3.5 lbs)	350	45-60
Chicken Breast (boneless)	380	12-15
Chicken Breast (bone-in)	350	22-25
Chicken Drumsticks	380	23-25
Chicken Thighs (bone-in)	380	23-25
Chicken Tenders	350	8-12
Chicken Wings	380	22-25

Pork & Lamb	Temp(℉)	Time
Bacon	350	8-12
Lamb Chops	400	8-12
Pork Chops (1" boneless)	400	8-10
Pork Loin (2 lbs.)	360	18-21
Rack of Lamb (24-32 oz.)	375	22-25
Ribs	400	10-15
Sausages	380	10-15

Printed in Great Britain
by Amazon

16158525R00046